AWS Step Functions Developer Guide

A catalogue record for this book is available from the Hong Kong Public Libraries.

Published in Hong Kong by Samurai Media Limited.

Email: info@samuraimedia.org

ISBN 9789888408764

Contents

What Is AWS Step Functions?

AWS Step Functions is a web service that enables you to coordinate the components of distributed applications and microservices using visual workflows. You build applications from individual components that each perform a discrete function, or *task*, allowing you to scale and change applications quickly. Step Functions provides a reliable way to coordinate components and step through the functions of your application. Step Functions provides a graphical console to visualize the components of your application as a series of steps. It automatically triggers and tracks each step, and retries when there are errors, so your application executes in order and as expected, every time. Step Functions logs the state of each step, so when things do go wrong, you can diagnose and debug problems quickly.

Step Functions manages the operations and underlying infrastructure for you to ensure your application is available at any scale.

You can run your tasks on the AWS Cloud, on your own servers, or on any system that has access to AWS. Step Functions can be accessed and used with the Step Functions console, the AWS SDKs, or an HTTP API. This guide shows you how to develop, test, and troubleshoot your own state machine using these methods.

Overview of Step Functions

Here are some of the key features of AWS Step Functions:

- Step Functions is based on the concepts of tasks and state machines.
- You define state machines using the JSON-based Amazon States Language.
- The Step Functions console displays a graphical view of your state machine's structure, which provides you with a way to visually check your state machine's logic and monitor executions.

Supported Regions

Currently, Step Functions is supported only in the following regions:

- US East (Ohio)
- US East (N. Virginia)
- US West (Oregon)
- US West (N. California)
- Asia Pacific (Sydney)
- Asia Pacific (Tokyo)
- Asia Pacific (Seoul)
- EU (Frankfurt)
- EU (Ireland)
- EU (London)
- Canada (Central)
- Asia Pacific (Singapore)

About Amazon Web Services

Amazon Web Services (AWS) is a collection of digital infrastructure services that developers can leverage when developing their applications. The services include computing, storage, database, and application synchronization (messaging and queuing). AWS uses a pay-as-you-go service model: you are charged only for the services that you—or your applications—use. For new AWS users, a free usage tier is available. On this tier, services are free below a certain level of usage. For more information about AWS costs and the Free Tier, see Use the AWS Free Tier. To obtain an AWS account, visit the AWS home page and choose **Create a Free Account**.

Getting Started

This tutorial introduces you to the basics of working with AWS Step Functions. You'll create a simple, independently running state machine using a **Pass** state. The **Pass** state represents a *no-op* (an instruction with no operation).

Topics

- Step 1: Creating a State Machine
- Step 2: Starting a New Execution
- Update a State Machine
- Next Steps

Step 1: Creating a State Machine

Step Functions offers various predefined state machines as *templates*. Create your first state machine using the **Hello World** template.

To create the state machine

1. Sign in to the Step Functions console, and then choose **Get Started**.

2. On the **Create a state machine** page, select **Templates** and then choose **Hello world**.

 Hello world

A basic example using a Pass state.

Step Functions fills in the name of the state machine automatically. It also populates the **Code** pane with the Amazon States Language description of the state machine.

```
1  {
2    "Comment": "A Hello World example of the Amazon States Language using a Pass state",
3    "StartAt": "HelloWorld",
4    "States": {
5      "HelloWorld": {
6        "Type": "Pass",
7        "Result": "Hello World!",
8        "End": true
9      }
10   }
11 }
```

This JSON text defines a **Pass** state named `HelloWorld`. For more information, see State Machine Structure.

3. Use the graph in the **Visual Workflow** pane to check that your Amazon States Language code describes your state machine correctly.

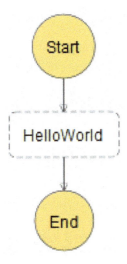

If you don't see the graph, choose ⟳ in the **Visual Workflow** pane.

4. Create or enter an IAM role.

   - To create a new IAM role for Step Functions, choose **Create a role for me**, and then choose **I acknowledge that Step Functions will create an IAM role which allows access to my Lambda functions.**
   - If you have previously created an IAM role for Step Functions, choose **I will provide an IAM role ARN** and enter your existing **IAM role ARN**. **Note**
     If you delete the IAM role that Step Functions creates, Step Functions can't recreate it later. Similarly, if you modify the role (for example, by removing Step Functions from the principals in the IAM policy), Step Functions can't restore its original settings later.

5. Choose **Create State Machine**.

Step 2: Starting a New Execution

After you create your state machine, you can start an execution.

To start a new execution

1. On the *Helloworld* page, choose **New execution**.

   The **New execution** window is displayed.

2. (Optional) To help identify your execution, you can specify an ID for it in the **Enter an execution name** box. If you don't enter an ID, Step Functions generates a unique ID automatically. **Note**
   Step Functions allows you to create state machine, execution, and activity names that contain non-ASCII characters. These non-ASCII names don't work with Amazon CloudWatch. To ensure that you can track CloudWatch metrics, choose a name that uses only ASCII characters.

3. Choose **Start Execution**.

   A new execution of your state machine starts, and a new page showing your running execution is displayed.

4. (Optional) In the **Execution Details** section, choose the **Info** tab to view the **Execution Status** and the **Started** and **Closed** timestamps.

5. To view the results of your execution, choose the **Output** tab.

Execution details

Execution Status

⊘ Succeeded

Execution ARN

arn:aws:states:us-east-
1:▓▓▓▓▓▓▓▓▓:execution:LambdaStateMachine:HelloLambdaTest

▼ Input

```
{
    "who": "AWS Step Functions"
}
```

Started

May 18, 2018 11:13:25.778 AM

End Time

May 18, 2018 11:13:26.273 AM

▼ Output

"Hello, AWS Step Functions!"

Step 3: (Optional) Update a State Machine

You can update your state machine for future executions.

Note
State machine updates in Step Functions are *eventually consistent*. All executions within a few seconds will use the updated definition and `roleArn`. Executions started immediately after updating a state machine may use the previous state machine definition and `roleArn`.

To update a state machine

1. On the *Helloworld* page, choose **Edit**.

   The **Edit** page is displayed.

2. In the **Code** pane, edit the Amazon States Language description of the state machine. Update the `Result` to read `Hello World has been updated!`

```
 1 {
 2   "Comment": "A Hello World example of the Amazon States Language using a Pass state",
 3   "StartAt": "HelloWorld",
 4   "States": {
 5     "HelloWorld": {
 6       "Type": "Pass",
 7       "Result": "Hello World has been updated!",
 8       "End": true
 9     }
10   }
11 }
```

3. (Optional) Select a new IAM role from the **IAM role for executions** list. **Note**
   You can also select **Create new role** to create a new IAM role. For more information, see Creating IAM Roles for AWS Step Functions.

4. Choose **Save** and then **Execute**.

5. On the **New execution** page choose **Start Execution**.

6. To view the results of your execution, select the **HelloWorld** state in the **Visual workflow** and expand the **Output** section under **Step details**.

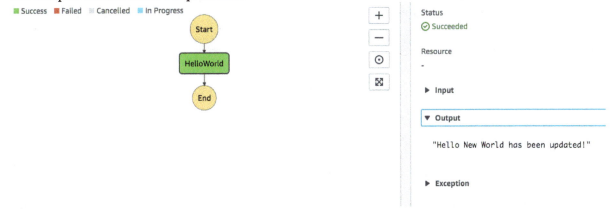

> **Note**
> The output text matches your newly updated state machine.

Next Steps

Now that you've created a simple state machine using a `Pass` state, try the following:

- Create a Lambda state machine
- Create a Lambda state machine using AWS CloudFormation
- Create an activity state machine
- Handle error conditions using a state machine
- Start a state machine using Amazon CloudWatch Events
- Create a Step Functions API using Amazon API Gateway

Tutorials

The following tutorials will help you get started working with AWS Step Functions. To complete these tutorials, you'll need an AWS account. If you don't have an AWS account, navigate to http://aws.amazon.com/ and choose **Sign In to the Console**.

Topics

- Development Options
- Creating a Lambda State Machine
- Creating a Lambda State Machine Using AWS CloudFormation
- Creating an Activity State Machine
- Handling Error Conditions Using a State Machine
- Starting a State Machine Execution Using CloudWatch Events
- Creating a Step Functions API Using API Gateway
- Iterating a Loop Using Lambda
- Continue as a New Execution

Development Options

You can implement your Step Functions state machines in a number of ways.

Step Functions Console

You can define a state machine using the Step Functions console. You can write complex state machines in the cloud without using a local development enviroment by taking advantage of Lambda to supply code for your tasks and the Step Functions console to define your state machine using Amazon States Language.

The Creating a Lambda State Machine tutorial uses this technique to create a simple state machine, execute it, and view its results.

AWS SDKs

Step Functions is supported by SDKs for Java, .NET, Ruby, PHP, Python (boto 3), JavaScript, Go, and C++, providing a convenient way to use the Step Functions HTTPS API actions in various programming languages.

You can develop state machines, activities, or state machine starters using the API actions exposed by these libraries. You can also access visibility operations using these libraries to develop your own Step Functions monitoring and reporting tools.

To use Step Functions with other AWS services, see the reference documentation for the current AWS SDKs and Tools for Amazon Web Services.

Note
Step Functions supports only an HTTPS endpoint.

HTTPS Service API

Step Functions provides service operations accessible through HTTPS requests. You can use these operations to communicate directly with Step Functions and to develop your own libraries in any language that can communicate with Step Functions through HTTPS.

You can develop state machines, workers, or state machine starters using the service API actions. You can also access visibility operations through the API actions to develop your own monitoring and reporting tools. For detailed information on API actions, see the *AWS Step Functions API Reference*.

Development Environments

You must set up a development environment appropriate to the programming language that you plan to use. For example, if you intend to develop for Step Functions with Java, you should install a Java development environment (such as the SDK for Java) on each of your development workstations. If you use Eclipse IDE for Java Development, you should also install the Toolkit for Eclipse. This Eclipse plug-in adds features useful for AWS development.

If your programming language requires a run-time environment, you must set up the environment on each computer where these processes run.

Endpoints

To reduce latency and to store data in a location that meets your requirements, Step Functions provides endpoints in different regions.

Each endpoint in Step Functions is completely independent: A state machine or activity exists only within the region where it was created. Any state machines and activities that you create in one region don't share any data or attributes with those created in another region. For example, you can register a state machine named `STATES-Flows-1` in two different regions, but the two state machines won't share data or attributes with each other, being completely independent from each other.

For a list of Step Functions endpoints, see Regions and Endpoints: AWS Step Functions in the *Amazon Web Services General Reference*.

AWS CLI

You can access many Step Functions features from the AWS CLI. The AWS CLI provides an alternative to using the Step Functions console or, in some cases, to program using the AWS Step Functions API actions. For example, you can use the AWS CLI to create a new state machine and then list your state machines.

The Step Functions commands in AWS CLI allow you to start and manage executions, poll for activities, record task heartbeats, and so on. For a complete list of Step Functions commands and the descriptions of the available arguments and examples showing their use, see the *AWS CLI Command Reference*.

The AWS CLI commands follow the Amazon States Language closely, so you can use the AWS CLI to learn about the Step Functions API actions. You can also use your existing API knowledge to prototype code or perform Step Functions actions from the command line.

Creating a Lambda State Machine

In this tutorial you'll create an AWS Step Functions state machine that uses a AWS Lambda function to implement a `Task` state. A `Task` state is a simple state that performs a single unit of work.

Lambda is well-suited for implementing `Task` states, because Lambda functions are *stateless* (they have a predictable input-output relationship), easy to write, and don't require deploying code to a server instance. You can write code in the AWS Management Console or your favorite editor, and AWS handles the details of providing a computing environment for your function and running it.

Topics

- Step 1: Creating an IAM Role for Lambda
- Step 2: Creating a Lambda Function
- Step 3: Testing the Lambda Function
- Step 4: Creating a State Machine
- Step 5: Starting a New Execution

Step 1: Creating an IAM Role for Lambda

Both Lambda and Step Functions can execute code and access AWS resources (for example, data stored in Amazon S3 buckets). To maintain security, you must grant Lambda and Step Functions access to these resources.

Lambda requires you to assign an IAM role when you create a Lambda function in the same way Step Functions requires you to assign an IAM role when you create a state machine.

To create a role for Lambda

You can use the IAM console to create a service-linked role.

To create a role (console)

1. Sign in to the AWS Management Console and open the IAM console at https://console.aws.amazon.com/iam/.

2. In the navigation pane of the IAM console, choose **Roles**. Then choose **Create role**.

3. Choose the **AWS Service** role type, and then choose **Lambda**.

4. Choose the **Lambda** use case. Use cases are defined by the service to include the trust policy required by the service. Then choose **Next: Permissions**.

5. Choose one or more permissions policies to attach to the role. Select the box next to the policy that assigns the permissions that you want the role to have, and then choose **Next: Review**.

6. Enter a **Role name**.

7. (Optional) For **Role description**, edit the description for the new service-linked role.

8. Review the role and then choose **Create role**.

Step 2: Creating a Lambda Function

Your Lambda function receives input (a name) and returns a greeting that includes the input value.

To create the Lambda function

Important
Ensure that your Lambda function is under the same AWS account and region as your state machine.

1. Log in to the Lambda console and choose **Create a function**.

2. In the **Blueprints** section, choose **Author from scratch**.

3. In the **Basic information** section, configure your Lambda function:

   1. For **Name**, type HelloFunction.

   2. For **Role**, select **Choose an existing role**.

   3. For **Existing role**, select the Lambda role that you created earlier. **Note**
      If the IAM role that you created doesn't appear in the list, the role might still need a few minutes to propagate to Lambda.

   4. Choose **Create function**.

      When your Lambda function is created, note its Amazon Resource Name (ARN) in the upper-right corner of the page. For example:

      ```
      1 arn:aws:lambda:us-east-1:123456789012:function:HelloFunction
      ```

4. Copy the following code for the Lambda function into the **Configuration** section of the *HelloFunction* page:

   ```
   1 exports.handler = (event, context, callback) => {
   2     callback(null, "Hello, " + event.who + "!");
   3 };
   ```

   This code assembles a greeting using the who field of the input data, which is provided by the event object passed into your function. You will add input data for this function later, when you start a new execution. The callback method returns the assembled greeting from your function.

5. Choose **Save**.

Step 3: Testing the Lambda Function

Test your Lambda function to see it in operation.

To test your Lambda function

1. On the **Select a test event** drop-down, choose **Configure test event** and type HelloFunction for **Event name**.

2. Replace the example data with the following:

   ```
   1 {
   2     "who": "AWS Step Functions"
   3 }
   ```

   The "who" entry corresponds to the event.who field in your Lambda function, completing the greeting. You will use the same input data when running the function as a Step Functions task.

3. Choose **Create**.

4. On the *HelloFunction* page, **Test** your Lambda function using the new data.

   The results of the test are displayed at the top of the page. Expand **Details** to see the output.

Step 4: Creating a State Machine

Use the Step Functions console to create a state machine with a `Task` state. Add a reference to your Lambda function in the `Task` state. The Lambda function is invoked when an execution of the state machine reaches the `Task` state.

To create the state machine

1. Log in to the Step Functions console and choose **Create a state machine**.

2. On the **Create a state machine** page, select **Author from scratch** and enter a **Name your state machine**, for example `LambdaStateMachine`. **Note**
   State machine names must be 1–80 characters in length, must be unique for your account and region, and must not contain any of the following:
   Whitespace Wildcard characters (? *) Bracket characters (< > { } [ ]) Special characters (: ; , \ |
   ^ ~ $ # % & "\) Control characters \(\u0000\-\u001for\u007f\-\u009f`). Step Functions allows you to create state machine, execution, and activity names that contain non-ASCII characters. These non-ASCII names don't work with Amazon CloudWatch. To ensure that you can track CloudWatch metrics, choose a name that uses only ASCII characters.

3. Create or enter an IAM role.

   - To create a new IAM role for Step Functions, choose **Create a role for me**, and then choose **I acknowledge that Step Functions will create an IAM role which allows access to my Lambda functions.**
   - If you have previously created an IAM role for Step Functions, choose **I will provide an IAM role ARN** and enter your existing **IAM role ARN**. **Note**
     If you delete the IAM role that Step Functions creates, Step Functions can't recreate it later. Similarly, if you modify the role (for example, by removing Step Functions from the principals in the IAM policy), Step Functions can't restore its original settings later.

4. In the **State machine definition** pane, add the following state machine definition using the ARN of the Lambda function that you created earlier, for example:

```
 1  {
 2    "Comment": "A Hello World example of the Amazon States Language using an AWS Lambda
          function",
 3    "StartAt": "HelloWorld",
 4    "States": {
 5    "HelloWorld": {
 6      "Type": "Task",
 7      "Resource": "arn:aws:lambda:us-east-1:123456789012:function:HelloFunction",
 8      "End": true
 9    }
10   }
11  }
```

   This is a description of your state machine using the Amazon States Language. It defines a single `Task` state named `HelloWorld`. For more information, see State Machine Structure. **Note**
   You can also set up a `Retry` for `Task` states. For more information see Retrying After an Error

5. Use the graph in the **Visual Workflow** pane to check that your Amazon States Language code describes your state machine correctly.

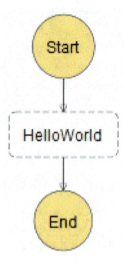

If you don't see the graph, choose ⟳ in the **Visual Workflow** pane.

6. Choose **Create State Machine**.

Step 5: Starting a New Execution

After you create your state machine, you can start an execution.

To start a new execution

1. On the *LambdaStateMachine* page, choose **Start execution**.

   The **New execution** page is displayed.

2. (Optional) To help identify your execution, you can specify an ID for it in the **Enter an execution name** box. If you don't enter an ID, Step Functions generates a unique ID automatically. **Note** Step Functions allows you to create state machine, execution, and activity names that contain non-ASCII characters. These non-ASCII names don't work with Amazon CloudWatch. To ensure that you can track CloudWatch metrics, choose a name that uses only ASCII characters.

3. In the execution input area, replace the example data with the following:

```
1 {
2     "who" : "AWS Step Functions"
3 }
```

   `"who"` is the key name that your Lambda function uses to get the name of the person to greet.

4. Choose **Start Execution**.

   A new execution of your state machine starts, and a new page showing your running execution is displayed.

5. To view the results of your execution, expand the **Output** section under **Execution details**.

Execution details

Execution Status

⊘ Succeeded

Execution ARN

arn:aws:states:us-east-1:~~~~~~~~~~~~:execution:LambdaStateMachine:HelloLambdaTest

▼ **Input**

```
{
  "who": "AWS Step Functions"
}
```

Started

May 18, 2018 11:13:25.778 AM

End Time

May 18, 2018 11:13:26.273 AM

▼ **Output**

```
"Hello, AWS Step Functions!"
```

Creating a Lambda State Machine Using AWS CloudFormation

This tutorial shows you how to create a basic AWS Lambda function and start a state machine execution automatically. You will use the AWS CloudFormation console and a YAML *template* to create the *stack* (IAM roles, the Lambda function, and the state machine). You will then use the AWS Step Functions console to start the state machine execution. For more information, see Working with CloudFormation Templates and the [AWS::StepFunctions::StateMachine](http://docs.aws.amazon.com/AWSCloudFormation/latest/UserGuide/aws-resource-stepfunctions-statemachine.html) resource in the *AWS CloudFormation User Guide*.

Topics

- Step 1: Setting Up Your AWS CloudFormation Template
- Step 2: Using the AWS CloudFormation Template to Create a Lambda State Machine
- Step 3: Starting a State Machine Execution

Step 1: Setting Up Your AWS CloudFormation Template

Before you use the example YAML template, you should understand its separate parts.

To create an IAM role for Lambda

Define the trust policy associated with the IAM role for the Lambda function.

```
1  LambdaExecutionRole:
2    Type: "AWS::IAM::Role"
3    Properties:
4      AssumeRolePolicyDocument:
5        Version: "2012-10-17"
6        Statement:
7          - Effect: Allow
8            Principal:
9              Service: lambda.amazonaws.com
10           Action: "sts:AssumeRole"
```

To create a Lambda function

Define the following properties of the Lambda function which prints the message `Hello World`.

Important

Ensure that your Lambda function is under the same AWS account and region as your state machine.

```
1  MyLambdaFunction:
2    Type: "AWS::Lambda::Function"
3    Properties:
4      Handler: "index.handler"
5      Role: !GetAtt [ LambdaExecutionRole, Arn ]
6      Code:
7        ZipFile: |
8          exports.handler = (event, context, callback) => {
9              callback(null, "Hello World!");
10         };
11     Runtime: "nodejs4.3"
12     Timeout: "25"
```

To create an IAM role for the state machine execution

Define the trust policy associated with the IAM role for the state machine execution.

```
1  StatesExecutionRole:
2    Type: "AWS::IAM::Role"
3    Properties:
4      AssumeRolePolicyDocument:
5        Version: "2012-10-17"
6        Statement:
7          - Effect: "Allow"
8            Principal:
9              Service:
10               - !Sub states.${AWS::Region}.amazonaws.com
11           Action: "sts:AssumeRole"
12     Path: "/"
13     Policies:
14       - PolicyName: StatesExecutionPolicy
15         PolicyDocument:
16           Version: "2012-10-17"
17           Statement:
18             - Effect: Allow
19               Action:
20                 - "lambda:InvokeFunction"
21               Resource: "*"
```

To create a Lambda state machine

Define the Lambda state machine.

```
1  MyStateMachine:
2    Type: "AWS::StepFunctions::StateMachine"
3    Properties:
4      DefinitionString:
5        !Sub
6        - |-
7          {
8            "Comment": "A Hello World AWL example using an AWS Lambda function",
9            "StartAt": "HelloWorld",
10           "States": {
11             "HelloWorld": {
12               "Type": "Task",
13               "Resource": "${lambdaArn}",
14               "End": true
15             }
16           }
17         }
18       - {lambdaArn: !GetAtt [ MyLambdaFunction, Arn ]}
19     RoleArn: !GetAtt [ StatesExecutionRole, Arn ]
```

Step 2: Using the AWS CloudFormation Template to Create a Lambda State Machine

After you understand the different parts of the AWS CloudFormation template, you can put them together and use the template to create a AWS CloudFormation stack.

To create the Lambda state machine

1. Copy the following example YAML data to a file named MyStateMachine.yaml.

```yaml
1  AWSTemplateFormatVersion: "2010-09-09"
2  Description: "An example template with an IAM role for a Lambda state machine."
3  Resources:
4    LambdaExecutionRole:
5      Type: "AWS::IAM::Role"
6      Properties:
7        AssumeRolePolicyDocument:
8          Version: "2012-10-17"
9          Statement:
10           - Effect: Allow
11             Principal:
12               Service: lambda.amazonaws.com
13             Action: "sts:AssumeRole"
14
15   MyLambdaFunction:
16     Type: "AWS::Lambda::Function"
17     Properties:
18       Handler: "index.handler"
19       Role: !GetAtt [ LambdaExecutionRole, Arn ]
20       Code:
21         ZipFile: |
22           exports.handler = (event, context, callback) => {
23               callback(null, "Hello World!");
24           };
25       Runtime: "nodejs4.3"
26       Timeout: "25"
27
28   StatesExecutionRole:
29     Type: "AWS::IAM::Role"
30     Properties:
31       AssumeRolePolicyDocument:
32         Version: "2012-10-17"
33         Statement:
34           - Effect: "Allow"
35             Principal:
36               Service:
37                 - !Sub states.${AWS::Region}.amazonaws.com
38             Action: "sts:AssumeRole"
39       Path: "/"
40       Policies:
41         - PolicyName: StatesExecutionPolicy
42           PolicyDocument:
43             Version: "2012-10-17"
44             Statement:
```

```
45        - Effect: Allow
46            Action:
47                - "lambda:InvokeFunction"
48            Resource: "*"
49
50   MyStateMachine:
51     Type: "AWS::StepFunctions::StateMachine"
52     Properties:
53       DefinitionString:
54         !Sub
55           - |-
56             {
57                "Comment": "A Hello World AWL example using an AWS Lambda function",
58                "StartAt": "HelloWorld",
59                "States": {
60                  "HelloWorld": {
61                    "Type": "Task",
62                    "Resource": "${lambdaArn}",
63                    "End": true
64                  }
65                }
66             }
67           - {lambdaArn: !GetAtt [ MyLambdaFunction, Arn ]}
68       RoleArn: !GetAtt [ StatesExecutionRole, Arn ]
```

2. Log in to the AWS CloudFormation console and choose **Create Stack**.

3. On the **Select Template** page, select **Upload a template to Amazon S3**. Choose your MyStateMachine.yaml file, and then choose **Next**.

4. On the **Specify Details** page, for **Stack name**, type MyStateMachine, and then choose **Next**.

5. On the **Options** page, choose **Next**.

6. On the **Review** page, choose **I acknowledge that AWS CloudFormation might create IAM resources.** and then choose **Create**.

   AWS CloudFormation begins to create the MyStateMachine stack and displays the **CRE-ATE_IN_PROGRESS** status. When the process is complete, AWS CloudFormation displays the **CREATE_COMPLETE** status.

7. (Optional) To display the resources in your stack, select the stack and choose the **Resources** tab.

Step 3: Starting a State Machine Execution

After you create your Lambda state machine, you can start an execution.

To start the state machine execution

1. Log in to the Step Functions console and choose the name of the state machine that you created using AWS CloudFormation.

2. On the *MyStateMachine-ABCDEFGHIJ1K* page, choose **New execution**.

   The **New execution** page is displayed.

3. (Optional) To help identify your execution, you can specify an ID for it in the **Enter an execution name** box. If you don't enter an ID, Step Functions generates a unique ID automatically. **Note** Step Functions allows you to create state machine, execution, and activity names that contain non-ASCII characters. These non-ASCII names don't work with Amazon CloudWatch. To ensure that you can track CloudWatch metrics, choose a name that uses only ASCII characters.

4. Choose **Start Execution**.

   A new execution of your state machine starts, and a new page showing your running execution is displayed.

5. (Optional) In the **Execution Details** section, choose the **Info** tab to view the **Execution Status** and the **Started** and **Closed** timestamps.

6. To view the results of your execution, choose the **Output** tab.

Execution details

Execution Status

⊘ Succeeded

Execution ARN

arn:aws:states:us-east-
1:▆▆▆▆▆▆▆:execution:LambdaStateMachine:HelloLambdaTest

▼ Input

```
{
  "who": "AWS Step Functions"
}
```

Started

May 18, 2018 11:13:25.778 AM

End Time

May 18, 2018 11:13:26.273 AM

▼ Output

```
"Hello, AWS Step Functions!"
```

Creating an Activity State Machine

You can coordinate task code in your state machine. This tutorial introduces you to creating an activity-based state machine using Java and AWS Step Functions.

To complete this tutorial you'll need the following:

- The SDK for Java. The example activity in this tutorial is a Java application that uses the AWS SDK for Java to communicate with AWS.
- AWS credentials in the environment or in the standard AWS configuration file. For more information, see Set up Your AWS credentials in the *AWS SDK for Java Developer Guide*.

Topics

- Step 1: Creating a New Activity
- Step 2: Creating a State Machine
- Step 3: Implementing a Worker
- Step 4: Starting an Execution
- Step 5: Running and Stopping the Worker

Step 1: Creating a New Activity

You must make Step Functions aware of the *activity* whose *worker* (a program) you want to create. Step Functions responds with an ARN that establishes an identity for the activity. Use this identity to coordinate the information passed between your state machine and worker.

Important
Ensure that your activity task is under the same AWS account as your state machine.

To create the new activity task

1. In the Step Functions console, choose **Activities** in the left navigation panel.

2. Choose **Create activity**.

3. Type an **Activity Name**. For example get-greeting, and choose **Create Activity**.

4. When your activity task is created, note its Amazon Resource Name (ARN), for example:

```
1 arn:aws:states:us-east-1:123456789012:activity:get-greeting
```

Step 2: Creating a State Machine

Create a state machine that will determine when your activity is invoked and when your worker should perform its primary work, collect its results, and return them.

To create the state machine

1. In the Step Functions console, choose **State machines** in the left navigation panel.

2. On the **State machines** page, choose **Create state machine**, select **Author from scratch**, and enter a name under **Details** (for example ActivityStateMachine). **Note**
State machine names must be 1–80 characters in length, must be unique for your account and region, and must not contain any of the following:

Whitespace Wildcard characters (? *) Bracket characters (< > { } [ ]) Special characters (: ; , \ |
^ ~ $ # % & "\) Control characters \(\u0000\-\u001for\u007f\-\u009f'). Step Functions allows
you to create state machine, execution, and activity names that contain non-ASCII characters. These
non-ASCII names don't work with Amazon CloudWatch. To ensure that you can track CloudWatch
metrics, choose a name that uses only ASCII characters.

3. Create or enter an IAM role.

- To create a new IAM role for Step Functions, choose **Create a role for me**, and then choose
  **I acknowledge that Step Functions will create an IAM role which allows access to my
  Lambda functions.**
- If you have previously created an IAM role for Step Functions, choose **I will provide an IAM role
  ARN** and enter your existing **IAM role ARN**. **Note**
  If you delete the IAM role that Step Functions creates, Step Functions can't recreate it later. Similarly,
  if you modify the role (for example, by removing Step Functions from the principals in the IAM
  policy), Step Functions can't restore its original settings later.

4. Under **State machine definition**, enter the following code, and include the ARN of the activity task
   that you created earlier in the `Resource` field, for example:

```
1  {
2    "Comment": "An example using a Task state.",
3    "StartAt": "getGreeting",
4    "Version": "1.0",
5    "TimeoutSeconds": 300,
6    "States":
7    {
8      "getGreeting": {
9        "Type": "Task",
10       "Resource": "arn:aws:states:us-east-1:123456789012:activity:get-greeting",
11       "End": true
12     }
13   }
14 }
```

This is a description of your state machine using the Amazon States Language. It defines a single `Task`
state named `getGreeting`. For more information, see State Machine Structure.

5. Use the graph in the **Visual Workflow** pane to check that your Amazon States Language code describes
   your state machine correctly.

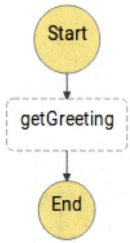

If you don't see the graph, choose ⟳ in the **Visual Workflow** pane.

6. Choose **Create State Machine**.

The state machine is created and an acknowledgement page is displayed.

Step 3: Implementing a Worker

Create a *worker*, a program which is responsible for the following:

- Polling Step Functions for activities using the `GetActivityTask` API action.
- Performing the work of the activity using your code, (for example, the `getGreeting()` method in the code below).
- Returning the results using the `SendTaskSuccess`, `SendTaskFailure`, and `SendTaskHeartbeat` API actions.

Note

For a more complete example of an activity worker, see Example Activity Worker in Ruby. This example provides an implementation based on best practices, that can be used as a reference for your activity worker. The code implements a consumer-producer pattern with a configurable number of threads for pollers and activity workers.

To implement the worker

1. Create a new file named `GreeterActivities.java`.

2. Add the following code to it:

```
1  import com.amazonaws.ClientConfiguration;
2  import com.amazonaws.auth.EnvironmentVariableCredentialsProvider;
3  import com.amazonaws.regions.Regions;
4  import com.amazonaws.services.stepfunctions.AWSStepFunctions;
5  import com.amazonaws.services.stepfunctions.AWSStepFunctionsClientBuilder;
6  import com.amazonaws.services.stepfunctions.model.GetActivityTaskRequest;
7  import com.amazonaws.services.stepfunctions.model.GetActivityTaskResult;
8  import com.amazonaws.services.stepfunctions.model.SendTaskFailureRequest;
9  import com.amazonaws.services.stepfunctions.model.SendTaskSuccessRequest;
10 import com.amazonaws.util.json.Jackson;
11 import com.fasterxml.jackson.databind.JsonNode;
12 import java.util.concurrent.TimeUnit;
13
14
15 public class GreeterActivities {
16
17     public String getGreeting(String who) throws Exception {
18         return "{\"Hello\": \"" + who + "\"}";
19     }
20
21     public static void main(final String[] args) throws Exception {
22         GreeterActivities greeterActivities = new GreeterActivities();
23         ClientConfiguration clientConfiguration = new ClientConfiguration();
24         clientConfiguration.setSocketTimeout((int)TimeUnit.SECONDS.toMillis(70));
25
26         AWSStepFunctions client = AWSStepFunctionsClientBuilder.standard()
27                 .withRegion(Regions.US_EAST_1)
28                 .withCredentials(new EnvironmentVariableCredentialsProvider())
29                 .withClientConfiguration(clientConfiguration)
30                 .build();
31
```

```
32        while (true) {
33            GetActivityTaskResult getActivityTaskResult =
34                    client.getActivityTask(
35                            new GetActivityTaskRequest().withActivityArn(ACTIVITY_ARN));
36
37            if (getActivityTaskResult.getTaskToken() != null) {
38                try {
39                    JsonNode json = Jackson.jsonNodeOf(getActivityTaskResult.getInput());
40                    String greetingResult =
41                            greeterActivities.getGreeting(json.get("who").textValue());
42                    client.sendTaskSuccess(
43                            new SendTaskSuccessRequest().withOutput(
44                                    greetingResult).withTaskToken(getActivityTaskResult.
                                        getTaskToken()));
45                } catch (Exception e) {
46                    client.sendTaskFailure(new SendTaskFailureRequest().withTaskToken(
47                            getActivityTaskResult.getTaskToken()));
48                }
49            } else {
50                Thread.sleep(1000);
51            }
52        }
53    }
54 }
```

Note

The `EnvironmentVariableCredentialsProvider` class in this example assumes that the `AWS_ACCESS_KEY_ID` (or `AWS_ACCESS_KEY`) and `AWS_SECRET_KEY` (or `AWS_SECRET_ACCESS_KEY`) environment variables are set. For more information about providing the required credentials to the factory, see AWSCredentialsProvider in the *AWS SDK for Java API Reference* and Set up AWS Credentials and Region for Development in the *AWS SDK for Java Developer Guide*.

To give Step Functions sufficient time to process the request, `setSocketTimeout` is set to 70 seconds.

1. In the parameter list of the `GetActivityTaskRequest().withActivityArn()` constructor, replace the `ACTIVITY_ARN` value with the ARN of the activity task that you created earlier.

Step 4: Starting an Execution

When you start the execution of the state machine, your worker polls Step Functions for activities, performs its work (using the input that you provide), and returns its results.

To start the execution

1. On the *ActivityStateMachine* page, choose **Start execution**.

   The **New execution** page is displayed.

2. (Optional) To help identify your execution, you can specify an ID for it in the **Enter an execution name** box. If you don't enter an ID, Step Functions generates a unique ID automatically. **Note**
   Step Functions allows you to create state machine, execution, and activity names that contain non-ASCII characters. These non-ASCII names don't work with Amazon CloudWatch. To ensure that you can track CloudWatch metrics, choose a name that uses only ASCII characters.

3. In the execution input area, replace the example data with the following:

```
1 {
2     "who" : "AWS Step Functions"
3 }
```

4. Choose **Start Execution**.

   A new execution of your state machine starts, and a new page showing your running execution is displayed.

5. In the **Execution Details** section, choose **Info** to view the **Execution Status** and the **Started** and **Closed** timestamps.

6. In the **Execution Details** section, expand the **Output** section to view the output of your workflow.

Step 5: Running and Stopping the Worker

To have the worker poll your state machine for activities, you must run the worker.

Note
After the execution completes, you should stop your worker. If you don't stop the worker, it will continue to run and poll for activities. When the execution is stopped, your worker has no source of tasks and generates a SocketTimeoutException during each poll.

To run and stop the worker

1. On the command line, navigate to the directory in which you created GreeterActivities.java.

2. To use the AWS SDK, add the full path of the lib and third-party directories to the dependencies of your build file and to your Java CLASSPATH. For more information, see Downloading and Extracting the SDK in the *AWS SDK for Java Developer Guide*.

3. Compile the file:

```
1 $ javac GreeterActivities.java
```

4. Run the file:

```
1 $ java GreeterActivities
```

5. In the Step Functions console, navigate to the **Execution Details** page.

6. When the execution completes, choose **Output** to see the results of your execution.

7. Stop the worker.

Handling Error Conditions Using a State Machine

In this tutorial, you create an AWS Step Functions state machine with a `Catch` field which uses an AWS Lambda function to respond with conditional logic based on error message type, a method called *function error handling*. For more information, see Function Error Handling in the *AWS Lambda Developer Guide*.

Note
You can also create state machines that `Retry` on timeouts or those that use `Catch` to transition to a specific state when an error or timeout occurs. For examples of these error handling techniques, see Examples Using Retry and Using Catch.

Topics

- Step 1: Creating an IAM Role for Lambda
- Step 2: Creating a Lambda Function That Fails
- Step 3: Testing the Lambda Function
- Step 4: Creating a State Machine with a `Catch` Field
- Step 5: Starting a New Execution

Step 1: Creating an IAM Role for Lambda

Both Lambda and Step Functions can execute code and access AWS resources (for example, data stored in Amazon S3 buckets). To maintain security, you must grant Lambda and Step Functions access to these resources.

Lambda requires you to assign an IAM role when you create a Lambda function in the same way Step Functions requires you to assign an IAM role when you create a state machine.

To create a role for Lambda

1. Sign in to the IAM console and choose **Roles, Create role**.

2. On the **Select type of trusted entity** page, under **AWS service**, select **Lambda** from the list, and then choose **Next: Permissions**. **Note**
   The role is automatically provided with a trust relationship that allows Lambda to use the role.

3. On the **Attach permissions policy** page, choose **Next: Review**.

4. On the **Review** page, type `MyLambdaRole` for **Role Name**, and then choose **Create role**.

The IAM role appears in the list of roles.

Step 2: Creating a Lambda Function That Fails

Use a Lambda function to simulate an error condition.

Important
Ensure that your Lambda function is under the same AWS account and region as your state machine.

To create a Lambda function that fails

1. Log in to the Lambda console and choose **Create a function**.

2. In the **Blueprints** section, type `step-functions` into the filter, and then choose the **step-functions-error** blueprint.

3. In the **Basic information** section, configure your Lambda function:

1. For **Name**, type `FailFunction`.

2. For **Role**, select **Choose an existing role**.

3. For **Existing role**, select the Lambda role that you created earlier. **Note**
   If the IAM role that you created doesn't appear in the list, the role might still need a few minutes to propagate to Lambda.

4. The following code is displayed in the **Lambda function code** pane:

```
1  'use strict';
2
3  exports.handler = (event, context, callback) => {
4      function CustomError(message) {
5          this.name = 'CustomError';
6          this.message = message;
7      }
8      CustomError.prototype = new Error();
9
10     const error = new CustomError('This is a custom error!');
11     callback(error);
12 };
```

The `context` object returns the error message `This is a custom error!`.

5. Choose **Create function**.

   When your Lambda function is created, note its Amazon Resource Name (ARN) in the upper-right corner of the page. For example:

```
1  arn:aws:lambda:us-east-1:123456789012:function:FailFunction
```

Step 3: Testing the Lambda Function

Test your Lambda function to see it in operation.

To test your Lambda function

1. On the *FailFunction* page, choose **Test**.
2. On the **Configure test event** dialog box, type `FailFunction` for **Event name**, and then choose **Create**.
3. On the *FailFunction* page, **Test** your Lambda function.

   The results of the test (the simulated error) are displayed at the bottom of the page.

Step 4: Creating a State Machine with a `Catch` Field

Use the Step Functions console to create a state machine that uses a `Task` state with a `Catch` field. Add a reference to your Lambda function in the `Task` state. The Lambda function is invoked and fails during execution. Step Functions retries the function twice using exponential backoff between retries.

To create the state machine

1. Log in to the Step Functions console and choose **Create state machine**.

2. On the **Create a state machine** page, select **Templates** and choose **Catch failure**.

 Catch failure
An example of a Task state using
Catchers to handle Lambda failures.

3. **Name your state machine**, for example `CatchStateMachine`. **Note**
State machine names must be 1–80 characters in length, must be unique for your account and region, and must not contain any of the following:
Whitespace Wildcard characters (? *) Bracket characters (< > { } [ ]) Special characters (: ; , \ | ^ ~ $ # % & "\) Control characters \(\u0000\-\u001for\u007f\-\u009f`). Step Functions allows you to create state machine, execution, and activity names that contain non-ASCII characters. These non-ASCII names don't work with Amazon CloudWatch. To ensure that you can track CloudWatch metrics, choose a name that uses only ASCII characters.

4. Create or enter an IAM role.

   - To create a new IAM role for Step Functions, choose **Create a role for me**, and then choose **I acknowledge that Step Functions will create an IAM role which allows access to my Lambda functions.**
   - If you have previously created an IAM role for Step Functions, choose **I will provide an IAM role ARN** and enter your existing **IAM role ARN**. **Note**
   If you delete the IAM role that Step Functions creates, Step Functions can't recreate it later. Similarly, if you modify the role (for example, by removing Step Functions from the principals in the IAM policy), Step Functions can't restore its original settings later.

5. In the **Code** pane, add the ARN of the Lambda function that you created earlier to the `Resource` field, for example:

```
1  {
2      "Comment": "A Catch example of the Amazon States Language using an AWS Lambda function",
3      "StartAt": "CreateAccount",
4      "States": {
5        "CreateAccount": {
6           "Type": "Task",
7           "Resource": "arn:aws:lambda:us-east-1:123456789012:function:FailFunction",
8           "Catch": [ {
9              "ErrorEquals": ["CustomError"],
10             "Next": "CustomErrorFallback"
11          }, {
12             "ErrorEquals": ["States.TaskFailed"],
13             "Next": "ReservedTypeFallback"
14          }, {
15             "ErrorEquals": ["States.ALL"],
16             "Next": "CatchAllFallback"
17          } ],
18          "End": true
19       },
20       "CustomErrorFallback": {
21          "Type": "Pass",
```

```
22        "Result": "This is a fallback from a custom Lambda function exception",
23        "End": true
24      },
25      "ReservedTypeFallback": {
26        "Type": "Pass",
27        "Result": "This is a fallback from a reserved error code",
28        "End": true
29      },
30      "CatchAllFallback": {
31        "Type": "Pass",
32        "Result": "This is a fallback from any error code",
33        "End": true
34      }
35    }
36 }
```

This is a description of your state machine using the Amazon States Language. It defines a single `Task` state named `CreateAccount`. For more information, see State Machine Structure.

For more information about the syntax of the `Retry` field, see Retrying After an Error. **Note** Unhandled errors in Lambda are reported as `Lambda.Unknown` in the error output. These include out-of-memory errors, function timeouts, and hitting the concurrent Lambda invoke limit. You can match on `Lambda.Unknown`, `States.ALL`, or `States.TaskFailed` to handle these errors. For more information about Lambda `Handled` and `Unhandled` errors, see `FunctionError` in the AWS Lambda Developer Guide.

6. Use the graph in the **Visual Workflow** pane to check that your Amazon States Language code describes your state machine correctly.

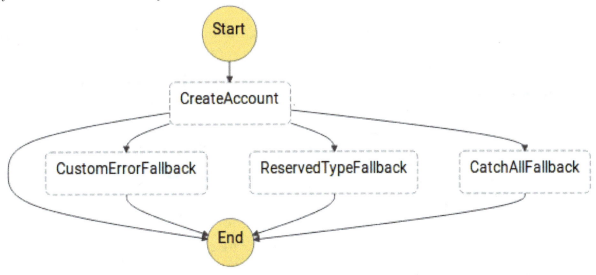

If you don't see the graph, choose ⟳ in the **Visual Workflow** pane.

7. Choose **Create State Machine**.

Step 5: Starting a New Execution

After you create your state machine, you can start an execution.

35

To start a new execution

1. On the *CatchStateMachine* page, choose **New execution**.

   The **New execution** page is displayed.

2. (Optional) To help identify your execution, you can specify an ID for it in the **Enter an execution name** box. If you don't enter an ID, Step Functions generates a unique ID automatically. **Note** Step Functions allows you to create state machine, execution, and activity names that contain non-ASCII characters. These non-ASCII names don't work with Amazon CloudWatch. To ensure that you can track CloudWatch metrics, choose a name that uses only ASCII characters.

3. Choose **Start Execution**.

   A new execution of your state machine starts, and a new page showing your running execution is displayed.

4. In the **Execution Details** section, expand the **Output** section to view the output of your workflow.

   ▼ Output

   "This is a fallback from a custom Lambda function exception"

5. To view your custom error message, select `CreateAccount` in the **Visual workflow** and expand the **Output** section.

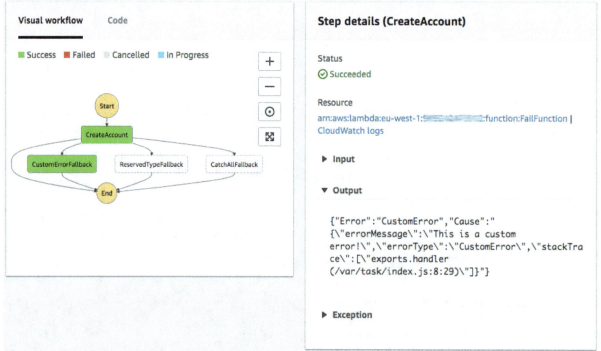

Note
You can preserve the state input along with the error by using `ResultPath`. See Use `ResultPath` to Include Both Error and Input in a `Catch`

Starting a State Machine Execution Using CloudWatch Events

You can execute a Step Functions state machine in response to an event pattern or on a schedule using Amazon CloudWatch Events. This tutorial shows how to set a state machine as a target for a CloudWatch Events rule that starts the execution of a state machine every 5 minutes.

For more information about setting a Step Functions state machine as a target using the `PutTarget` Amazon CloudWatch Events API action, see Add a Step Functions state machine as a target.

Topics

- Step 1: Creating a State Machine
- Step 2: Creating a CloudWatch Events Rule

Step 1: Creating a State Machine

Before you can set a CloudWatch Events target, you must create a state machine.

- To create a basic state machine, use the Getting Started tutorial.
- If you already have a state machine, proceed to the next step.

Step 2: Creating a CloudWatch Events Rule

After you create your state machine, you can create your CloudWatch Events rule.

To create the rule

1. Navigate to the CloudWatch Events console, choose **Events**, and then choose **Create Rule**.

   The **Step 1: Create rule** page is displayed.

2. In the **Event source** section, select **Schedule** and type 5 for **Fixed rate of**.

3. In the **Targets** section, choose **Add target** and from the list choose **Step Functions state machine**.

Targets

Select Target to invoke when an event matches your Event Pattern or when schedule is triggered

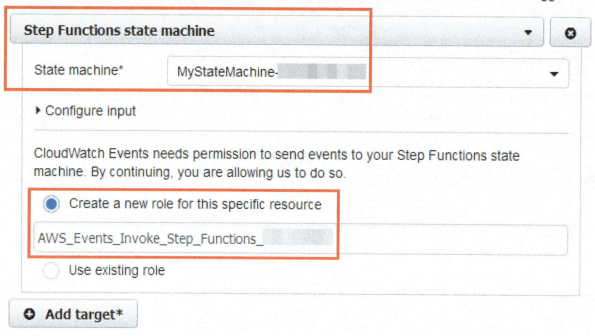

● Add target*

4. CloudWatch Events can create the IAM role needed for your event to run:

   - To create an IAM role automatically, select **Create a new role for this specific resource**.
   - To use an IAM role that you created before, choose **Use existing role**.

5. Choose **Configure details**.

   The **Step 2: Configure rule details** page is displayed.

6. Type a **Name** for your rule (for example, `statemachine-event`), choose **Enabled** for **State**, and then choose **Create rule**.

Rule definition

The rule is created and the **Rules** page is displayed, listing all your CloudWatch Events rules.

Rules

Rules route events from your AWS resources for processing by selected targets. You can create, edit, and delete rules.

A new execution of your state machine starts every 5 minutes.

Creating a Step Functions API Using API Gateway

You can use Amazon API Gateway to associate your AWS Step Functions APIs with methods in an API Gateway API, so that, when an HTTPS request is sent to an API method, API Gateway invokes your Step Functions API actions.

This tutorial shows you how to create an API that uses one resource and the POST method to communicate with the StartExecution API action. You'll use the IAM console to create a role for API Gateway. Then, you'll use the API Gateway console to create an API Gateway API, create a resource and method, and map the method to the StartExecution API action. Finally, you'll deploy and test your API. For more information about this API action, see StartExecution in the *AWS Step Functions API Reference*.

Topics

- Step 1: Creating an IAM Role for API Gateway
- Step 2: Creating your API Gateway API
- Step 3: Testing and Deploying the API Gateway API

Step 1: Creating an IAM Role for API Gateway

Before you create your API Gateway API, you need to give API Gateway permission to call Step Functions API actions.

To create a role for API Gateway

1. Log in to the IAM console and choose **Roles, Create role**.

2. On the **Select type of trusted entity** page, under **AWS service**, select **API Gateway** from the list and then choose **Next: Permissions**.

3. On the **Attached permissions policy** page, choose **Next: Review**.

4. On the **Review** page, type APIGatewayToStepFunctions for **Role name** and then choose **Create role**.

   The IAM role appears in the list of roles.

5. Choose the name of your role and note the **Role ARN**, for example:

```
1  arn:aws:iam::123456789012:role/APIGatewayToStepFunctions
```

To attach a policy to the IAM role

1. On the **Roles** page, search for your role (APIGatewayToStepFunctions) and then choose the role.

2. On the **Permissions** tab, choose **Attach Policy**.

3. On the **Attach Policy** page, search for AWSStepFunctionsFullAccess, choose the policy, and then choose **Attach Policy**.

Step 2: Creating your API Gateway API

After you create your IAM role, you can create your custom API Gateway API.

To create the API

1. Navigate to the Amazon API Gateway console and choose **Get Started**.

2. On the **Create new API** page, choose **New API**.

3. In the **Settings** section, type `StartExecutionAPI` for the **API name**, and then choose **Create API**.

To create a resource

1. On the **Resources** page of *StartExecutionAPI*, choose **Actions**, **Create Resource**.

2. On the **New Child Resource** page, type `execution` for **Resource Name**, and then choose **Create Resource**.

To create a POST Method

1. On the **/execution Methods** page, choose **Actions**, **Create Method**.

2. From the list, choose `POST`, and then select the checkmark.

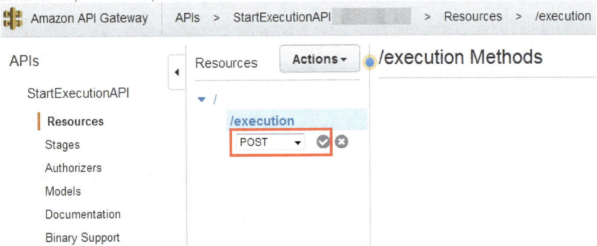

To configure the method

On the **/execution - POST - Setup** page, configure the integration point for your method.

1. For **Integration Type**, choose **AWS Service**.

2. For **AWS Region**, choose a region from the list. **Note**
   For regions that currently support Step Functions, see the Supported Regions.

3. For **AWS Service**, choose **Step Functions** from the list.

4. For **HTTP Method**, choose **POST** from the list. **Note**
   All Step Functions API actions use the HTTP `POST` method.

5. For **Action Type**, choose **Use action name**.

6. For **Action**, type `StartExecution`.

7. For **Execution Role**, type the role ARN of the IAM role that you created earlier, for example:

```
1 arn:aws:iam::123456789012:role/APIGatewayToStepFunctions
```

/execution - POST - Setup

Choose the integration point for your new method.

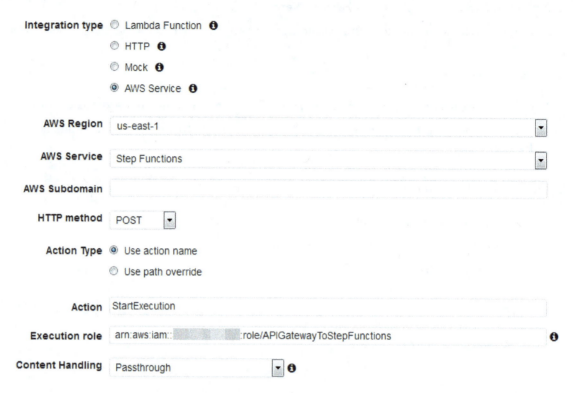

Integration type ○ Lambda Function ❶
　　　　　　　　　　 ○ HTTP ❶
　　　　　　　　　　 ○ Mock ❶
　　　　　　　　　　 ◉ AWS Service ❶

AWS Region us-east-1 ▾

AWS Service Step Functions ▾

AWS Subdomain

HTTP method POST ▾

Action Type ◉ Use action name
　　　　　　　　 ○ Use path override

Action StartExecution

Execution role arn:aws:iam:: :role/APIGatewayToStepFunctions ❶

Content Handling Passthrough ▾ ❶

1. Choose **Save**.

   The visual mapping between API Gateway and Step Functions is displayed on the **/execution - POST - Method Execution** page.

   /execution - POST - Method Execution

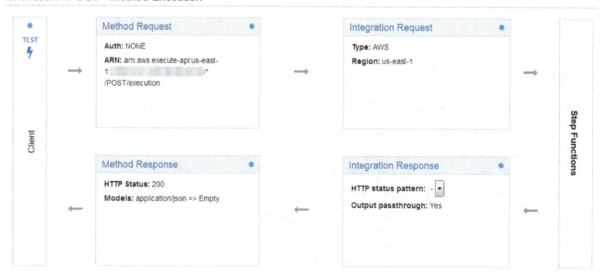

Step 3: Testing and Deploying the API Gateway API

To test the communication between API Gateway and Step Functions

1. On the **/execution - POST - Method Execution** page, choose **Test**.

2. On the **/execution - POST - Method Test** page, copy the following request parameters into the **Request Body** section using the ARN of an existing state machine (or create a new state machine), and then choose **Test**.

```
1 {
2     "input": "{}",
3     "name": "MyExecution",
4     "stateMachineArn": "arn:aws:states:us-east-1:123456789012:stateMachine:HelloWorld"
5 }
```

Note

For more information, see the `StartExecution` Request Syntax in the *AWS Step Functions API Reference*.
If you don't want to include the ARN of your state machine in the body of your API Gateway call, you can configure a body-mapping template, for example:

```
1 {
2     "input": "$util.escapeJavaScript($input.json('$'))",
3     "stateMachineArn": "arn:aws:states:us-east-1:123456789012:stateMachine:HelloWorld"
4 }
```

This approach allows you to have different state machines based on your development stages (for example, `dev`, `test`, and `prod`). To release an update, you only need to change the stage variable, for example:

```
1 {
2     "input": "$util.escapeJavaScript($input.json('$'))",
3     "stateMachineArn": "$util.escapeJavaScript($stageVariables.get(arn:aws:states:us-east
          -1:123456789012:stateMachine:HelloWorld))"
4 }
```

1. The execution starts and the execution ARN and its epoch date are displayed under **Response Body**.

```
1 {
2     "executionArn": "arn:aws:states:us-east-1:123456789012:execution:HelloWorld:MyExecution
          ",
3     "startDate": 1486768956.878
4 }
```

Note

You can view the execution by choosing your state machine on the AWS Step Functions console.

To deploy your API

1. On the **Resources** page of *StartExecutionAPI*, choose **Actions**, **Deploy API**.

2. In the **Deploy API** dialog box, select [**New Stage**] from the **Deployment stage** list, type `alpha` for **Stage name**, and then choose **Deploy**.

To test your deployment

1. On the **Stages** page of *StartExecutionAPI*, expand **alpha**, /, /execution, **POST**.

2. On the **alpha - POST - /execution** page, note the **Invoke URL**, for example:

```
1 https://a1b2c3d4e5.execute-api.us-east-1.amazonaws.com/alpha/execution
```

3. From the command line, run the `curl` command using the ARN of your state machine, and then invoke the URL of your deployment, for example:

```
1 curl -X POST -d '{"input": "{}","name": "MyExecution","stateMachineArn": "arn:aws:states:us
      -east-1:123456789012:stateMachine:HelloWorld"}' https://a1b2c3d4e5.execute-api.us-east
      -1.amazonaws.com/alpha/execution
```

The execution ARN and its epoch date are returned, for example:

```
1 {"executionArn":"arn:aws:states:us-east-1:123456789012:execution:HelloWorld:MyExecution","
      startDate":1.486772644911E9}
```

Iterating a Loop Using Lambda

In this tutorial, you implement a design pattern that uses a state machine and an AWS Lambda function to iterate a loop a specific number of times.

Use this design pattern any time you need to keep track of the number of loops in a state machine. This implementation can help you break up large tasks or long-running executions into smaller chunks, or to end an execution after a specific number of events. You can use a similar implementation to periodically end and restart a long-running execution to avoid exceeding service limits for AWS Step Functions, AWS Lambda, or other AWS services.

Before you begin, go through the Creating a Lambda State Machine tutorial to ensure you have created the necessary IAM role, and are familiar with using Lambda and Step Functions together.

Topics

- Step 1: Create a Lambda Function to Iterate a Count
- Step 2: Test the Lambda Function
- Step 3: Create a State Machine
- Step 4: Start a New Execution

Step 1: Create a Lambda Function to Iterate a Count

By using a Lambda function you can track the number of iterations of a loop in your state machine. The following Lambda function receives input values for `count`, `index`, and `step`. It returns these values with an updated `index` and a Boolean named `continue`. The Lambda function sets `continue` to `true` if the `index` is less than `count`.

Your state machine then implements a `Choice` state that executes some application logic if `continue` is `true`, or exits if it is `false`.

To create the Lambda function

1. Sign in to the Lambda console, and then choose **Create function**.

2. In the **Create function** section, choose **Author from scratch**.

3. In the **Author from scratch** section, configure your Lambda function, as follows:

   1. For **Name**, type `Iterator`.

   2. For **Runtime**, select **Node.js 6.10**.

   3. For **Role**, select **Choose an existing role**.

   4. For **Existing role**, select the Lambda role that you created in the Creating a Lambda State Machine tutorial. **Note**
   If the IAM role that you created doesn't appear in the list, the role might still need a few minutes to propagate to Lambda.

   5. Choose **Create function**.

      When your Lambda function is created, make a note of its Amazon Resource Name (ARN) in the upper-right corner of the page. For example:

      ```
      1 arn:aws:lambda:us-east-1:123456789012:function:Iterator
      ```

4. Copy the following code for the Lambda function into the **Configuration** section of the *Iterator* page in the Lambda console.

```
1  exports.iterator = function iterator (event, context, callback) {
2    let index = event.iterator.index
3    let step = event.iterator.step
4    let count = event.iterator.count
5
6    index += step
7
8    callback(null, {
9      index,
10     step,
11     count,
12     continue: index < count
13   })
14 }
```

This code accepts input values for `count`, `index`, and `step`. It increments the `index` by the value of `step` and returns these values, and the Boolean `continue`. The value of `continue` is `true` if `index` is less than `count`.

5. Choose **Save**.

Step 2: Test the Lambda Function

Run your Lambda function with numeric values to see it in operation. You can provide input values for your Lambda function that mimic an iteration, to see what output you get with specific input values.

To test your Lambda function

1. In the **Configure test event** dialog box, choose **Create new test event**, and then type `TestIterator` for **Event name**.

2. Replace the example data with the following.

```
1  {
2    "Comment": "Test my Iterator function",
3    "iterator": {
4      "count": 10,
5      "index": 5,
6      "step": 1
7    }
8  }
```

These values mimic what would come from your state machine during an iteration. The Lambda function will increment the index and return `continue` as `true`. Once the index is not less than the `count`, it will return `continue` as `false`. For this test, the index has already incremented to 5. The results should increment the `index` to 6 and set `continue` to `true`.

3. Choose **Create**.

4. On the *Iterator* page in your Lambda console, be sure **TestIterator** is listed, and then choose **Test**.

   The results of the test are displayed at the top of the page. Choose **Details** and review the result.

```
1  {
2    "index": 6,
3    "step": 1,
4    "count": 10,
```

```
5    "continue": true
6 }
```

Note

If you set `index` to 9 for this test, the `index` will increment to 10, and `continue` will be `false`.

Step 3: Create a State Machine

To create the state machine

1. Sign in to the Step Functions console, and then choose **Create a state machine. Important**
   Ensure that your state machine is under the same AWS account and region as the Lambda function you
   created earlier.

2. On the **Create a state machine** page, choose **Author from scratch**. For **Give a name to your
   state machine**, enter `IterateCount`. **Note**
   State machine names must be 1–80 characters in length, must be unique for your account and region, and
   must not contain any of the following:
   Whitespace Wildcard characters (? *) Bracket characters (< > { } [ ]) Special characters (: ; , \ |
   ^ ~ $ # % & "\) Control characters \(\u0000\-\u001for\u007f\-\u009f`). Step Functions allows
   you to create state machine, execution, and activity names that contain non-ASCII characters. These
   non-ASCII names don't work with Amazon CloudWatch. To ensure that you can track CloudWatch
   metrics, choose a name that uses only ASCII characters.

3. Create or enter an IAM role.

   - To create a new IAM role for Step Functions, choose **Create a role for me**, and then choose
     **I acknowledge that Step Functions will create an IAM role which allows access to my
     Lambda functions.**
   - If you have previously created an IAM role for Step Functions, choose **I will provide an IAM role
     ARN** and enter your existing **IAM role ARN. Note**
     If you delete the IAM role that Step Functions creates, Step Functions can't recreate it later. Similarly,
     if you modify the role (for example, by removing Step Functions from the principals in the IAM
     policy), Step Functions can't restore its original settings later.

4. The following code describes a state machine with the following states:

   - ConfigureCount: Sets the default values for `count`, `index`, and `step`.

```
1 "ConfigureCount": {
2     "Type": "Pass",
3     "Result": {
4         "count": 10,
5         "index": 0,
6         "step": 1
7 },
```

   - Iterator: References your Lambda function you created earlier, passing in the values configured in
     ConfigureCount.

```
1 "Iterator": {
2     "Type": "Task",
3     "Resource": "arn:aws:lambda:us-east-1:123456789012:function:Iterate",
4     "ResultPath": "$.iterator",
5     "Next": "IsCountReached"
6 },
```

- **IsCountReached**: A choice state that will either run your sample work again or will go to **Done** based on a boolean returned from your **Iterator** Lambda function.

```
1  "IsCountReached": {
2      "Type": "Choice",
3      "Choices": [
4          {
5              "Variable": "$.iterator.continue",
6              "BooleanEquals": true,
7              "Next": "ExampleWork"
8          }
9      ],
10     "Default": "Done"
11 },
```

- **ExampleWork**: A stub for the work you want to accomplish in your execution. In this example it is a **pass** state. In an actual implementation this would be a **task** state. See Tasks.

- **Done**: The end state of your execution.

In the **Code** pane, add the following state machine definition using the Amazon Resource Name of the Lambda function that you created earlier.

```
1  {
2      "Comment": "Iterator State Machine Example",
3      "StartAt": "ConfigureCount",
4      "States": {
5
6          "ConfigureCount": {
7              "Type": "Pass",
8              "Result": {
9                  "count": 10,
10                 "index": 0,
11                 "step": 1
12             },
13             "ResultPath": "$.iterator",
14             "Next": "Iterator"
15         },
16         "Iterator": {
17             "Type": "Task",
18             "Resource": "arn:aws:lambda:us-east-1:123456789012:function:Iterate",
19             "ResultPath": "$.iterator",
20             "Next": "IsCountReached"
21         },
22         "IsCountReached": {
23             "Type": "Choice",
24             "Choices": [
25                 {
26                     "Variable": "$.iterator.continue",
27                     "BooleanEquals": true,
28                     "Next": "ExampleWork"
29                 }
30             ],
31             "Default": "Done"
32         },
33         "ExampleWork": {
34             "Comment": "Your application logic, to run a specific number of times",
```

```
35        "Type": "Pass",
36        "Result": {
37          "success": true
38        },
39        "ResultPath": "$.result",
40        "Next": "Iterator"
41      },
42      "Done": {
43        "Type": "Pass",
44        "End": true
45
46      }
47    }
48 }
```

Be sure to update the Amazon Resource Name in the `Iterator` state above so that it references the Lambda you created earlier. For more information about the Amazon States Language, see State Machine Structure.

5. Use the graph in the **Visual Workflow** pane to check that your Amazon States Language code describes your state machine correctly.

This graph shows the logic expressed in the above state machine code.

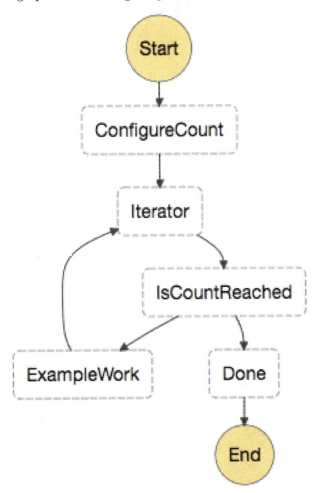

If you don't see the graph, choose in the **Visual Workflow** pane.

6. Choose **Create State Machine**.

7. Choose **OK**.

   The state machine is created and an acknowledgement page is displayed.

Step 4: Start a New Execution

After you create your state machine, you can start an execution.

To start a new execution

1. On the **IterateCount** page, choose **New execution**.

2. (Optional) To help identify your execution, you can specify an ID for it in the **Enter an execution name** box. If you don't enter an ID, Step Functions generates a unique ID automatically. **Note** Step Functions allows you to create state machine, execution, and activity names that contain non-ASCII characters. These non-ASCII names don't work with Amazon CloudWatch. To ensure that you can track CloudWatch metrics, choose a name that uses only ASCII characters.

3. Choose **Start Execution**.

   A new execution of your state machine starts, showing your running execution.

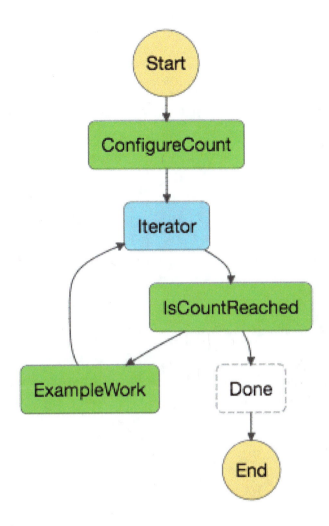

The execution increments in steps, tracking the count using your Lambda function. On each iteration, it performs the example work referenced in the `ExampleWork` state in your state machine.

4. (Optional) In the **Execution Details** section, choose the **Info** tab to view the **Execution Status** and the **Started** and **Closed** time stamps.

5. Once the count reaches the number configured in the `ConfigureCount` state in your state machine, the execution quits iterating and ends.

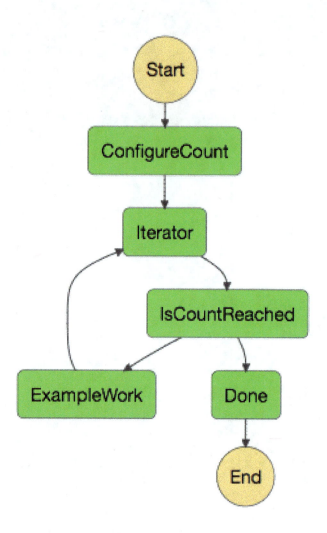

Continue as a New Execution

AWS Step Functions is designed to run workflows that have a finite duration and number of steps. Executions are limited to a duration of one year, and a maximum of 25,000 events (see Limits). However, you can create a state machine that uses a Lambda function to start a new execution, before allowing the current execution to terminate. This enables you to have a state machine that can break large jobs into smaller workflows, or to have a state machine that runs indefinitely.

This tutorial builds on the concept of using an external Lambda function to modify your workflow, which was demonstrated in the Iterating a Loop Using Lambda tutorial. You'll use the same Lambda function (`Iterator`) to iterate a loop for a specific number of times. In addition, you'll create another Lambda function to start a new execution of your workflow, and to decrement a count each time it starts a new execution. By setting the number of executions in the input, this state machine will end and restart an execution a specified number of times.

This tutorial shows you how to create a state machine with a Lambda function that can start a new execution, continuing your ongoing work in that new execution.

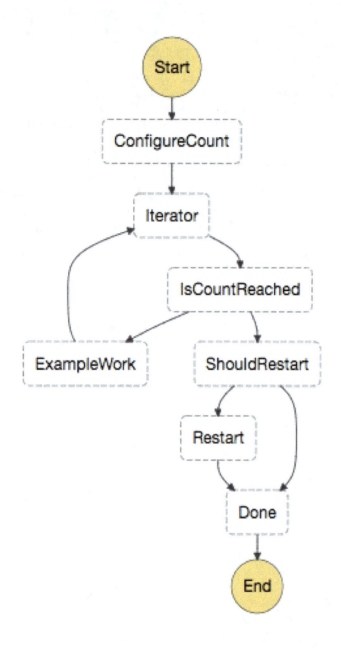

The state machine you'll create implements the following states.

State	Purpose
ConfigureCount	A [Pass](amazon-states-language-pass-state.md) state that configures the count, index, and step values that are used by the Iterator Lambda function to step through iterations of work.
Iterator	A [Task](amazon-states-language-task-state.md) state that references the Iterator Lambda function.

State	Purpose
IsCountReached	A Choice state that uses a Boolean value from the Iterator function to decide if the state machine should continue the example work, or move to the ShouldRestart choice state.
ExampleWork	In this example, ExampleWork is a Pass state that represents the Task state that would perform work in an actual implementation.
ShouldRestart	A Choice state that uses the executionCount value to decide if it should end one execution and start another, or simply end.
Restart	A Task state that uses a Lambda function to start a new execution of your state machine. Like the Iterator function, this function also decrements a count. It passes that value to the input of the new execution.

Prerequisites

Before you begin, go through the Creating a Lambda State Machine tutorial to ensure you have created an initial IAM role, and that you are familiar with using Lambda and Step Functions together.

Topics

- Prerequisites
- Step 1: Create an `Iterate` Lambda Function to Iterate a Count
- Step 2: Create a `Restart` Lambda Function to Start a New Step Functions Execution
- Step 3: Create a State Machine
- Step 4: Update the IAM Policy
- Step 5: Run an Execution

Step 1: Create an `Iterate` Lambda Function to Iterate a Count

Note
If you have completed the Iterating a Loop Using Lambda tutorial, you can skip this step and use that Lambda function.

This section, and the Iterating a Loop Using Lambda tutorial, shows how you can use a Lambda function to track a count so that you can track the number of iterations of a loop in your state machine.

The following Lambda function receives input values for `count`, `index`, and `step`. It returns these values with an updated `index` and a Boolean named `continue`. The Lambda function sets `continue` to `true` if the `index` is less than `count`.

Your state machine then implements a `Choice` state that executes some application logic if `continue` is `true`, or moves on to `ShouldRestart` if `continue` is `false`.

To create the `Iterate` Lambda function

1. Sign in to the Lambda console, and then choose **Create function**.

2. In the **Create function** section, choose **Author from scratch**.

3. In the **Author from scratch** section, configure your Lambda function, as follows:

1. For **Name**, type `Iterator`.

2. For **Runtime**, select **Node.js 6.10**.

3. For **Role**, select **Choose an existing role**.

4. For **Existing role**, select the Lambda role that you created in the Creating a Lambda State Machine tutorial. **Note**
   If the IAM role that you created doesn't appear in the list, the role might still need a few minutes to propagate to Lambda.

5. Choose **Create function**.

   When your Lambda function is created, make a note of its Amazon Resource Name (ARN) in the upper-right corner of the page. For example:

   ```
   1 arn:aws:lambda:us-east-1:123456789012:function:Iterator
   ```

4. Copy the following code for the Lambda function into the **Configuration** section of the *Iterator* page in the Lambda console.

```
1  exports.iterator = function iterator (event, context, callback) {
2    let index = event.iterator.index
3    let step = event.iterator.step
4    let count = event.iterator.count
5
6    index += step
7
8    callback(null, {
9      index,
10     step,
11     count,
12     continue: index < count
13   })
14 }
```

This code accepts input values for `count`, `index`, and `step`. It increments the `index` by the value of `step` and returns these values, and the Boolean `continue`. The value of `continue` is `true` if `index` is less than `count`.

5. Choose **Save**.

Test the `Iterate` Lambda Function

To see your `Iterate` function working, run it with numeric values. You can provide input values for your Lambda function that mimic an iteration to see what output you get with specific input values.

To test your Lambda function

1. In the **Configure test event** dialog box, choose **Create new test event**, and then type `TestIterator` for **Event name**.

2. Replace the example data with the following.

```
1 {
2   "Comment": "Test my Iterator function",
3   "iterator": {
4     "count": 10,
5     "index": 5,
```

```
6      "step": 1
7    }
8  }
```

These values mimic what would come from your state machine during an iteration. The Lambda function increments the index and returns `continue` as `true`. Once the index is not less than the `count`, it returns `continue` as `false`. For this test, the index has already incremented to 5. The results should increment the `index` to 6 and set `continue` to `true`.

3. Choose **Create**.

4. On the *Iterator* page in your Lambda console, be sure **TestIterator** is listed, and then choose **Test**.

   The results of the test are displayed at the top of the page. Choose **Details** and review the result.

```
1  {
2    "index": 6,
3    "step": 1,
4    "count": 10,
5    "continue": true
6  }
```

Note
If you set `index` to 9 for this test, the `index` increments to 10, and `continue` is `false`.

Step 2: Create a `Restart` Lambda Function to Start a New Step Functions Execution

1. Sign in to the Lambda console, and then choose **Create function**.

2. In the **Author from scratch** section, configure your Lambda function, as follows:

   1. For **Name**, type `Restart`.

   2. For **Runtime**, select **Node.js 6.10**.

   3. For **Role**, select **Choose an existing role**.

   4. Under **Existing role**, select the role that includes the IAM policy you created previously.

   5. Choose **Create function**.

      When your Lambda function is created, make a note of its Amazon Resource Name (ARN) in the upper-right corner of the page. For example:

```
1  arn:aws:lambda:us-east-1:123456789012:function:Restart
```

3. Copy the following code for the Lambda function into the **Configuration** section of the *Restart* page in the Lambda console.

   The following code decrements a count of the number of executions, and starts a new execution of your state machine, including the decremented value.

```
1  var aws = require('aws-sdk');
2  var sfn = new aws.StepFunctions();
3
4  exports.restart = function(event, context, callback) {
5
6    let StateMachineArn = event.restart.StateMachineArn;
7    event.restart.executionCount -= 1;
8    event = JSON.stringify(event);
```

```
 9
10    let params = {
11        input: event,
12        stateMachineArn: StateMachineArn
13    };
14
15    sfn.startExecution(params, function(err, data) {
16        if (err) callback(err);
17        else callback(null,event);
18    });
19
20 }
```

4. Choose **Save**.

Step 3: Create a State Machine

Now that you've created your two Lambda functions, create a state machine. In this state machine, the `ShouldRestart` and `Restart` states are how you break your work across multiple executions.

Example `ShouldRestart` Choice state
This excerpt of your state machine shows the `ShouldRestart` [Choice](amazon-states-language-choice-state.md) state. This state decides if you should restart the execution.

```
1 "ShouldRestart": {
2 "Type": "Choice",
3 "Choices": [
4   {
5     "Variable": "$.restart.executionCount",
6     "NumericGreaterThan": 1,
7     "Next": "Restart"
8   }
9 ],
```

The `$.restart.executionCount` value is included in the input of the initial execution. It's decremented by one each time the `Restart` function is called, and then placed into the input for each subsequent execution.

Example `Restart` Task state
This excerpt of your state machine shows the `Restart` [Task](amazon-states-language-task-state.md) state. This state uses the Lambda function you created earlier to restart the execution, and to decrement the count to track the remaining number of executions to start.

```
1 "Restart": {
2   "Type": "Task",
3   "Resource": "arn:aws:lambda:us-east-1:123456789012:function:Restart",
4   "Next": "Done"
5 },
```

1. In the Step Functions console, choose **Create a state machine**.

2. Select **Author from scratch**, and enter `ContinueAsNew` as your state machine name.

3. Under **IAM role for your state machine executions**, select the IAM role that you use for Lambda functions.

4. Paste the following into the `Code` pane.
   Example `ContinueAsNew` state machine

```json
{
    "Comment": "Continue-as-new State Machine Example",
    "StartAt": "ConfigureCount",
    "States": {
        "ConfigureCount": {
            "Type": "Pass",
            "Result": {
                "count": 100,
                "index": -1,
                "step": 1
            },
            "ResultPath": "$.iterator",
            "Next": "Iterator"
        },
        "Iterator": {
            "Type": "Task",
            "Resource": "arn:aws:lambda:us-east-1:123456789012:function:Iterator",
            "ResultPath": "$.iterator",
            "Next": "IsCountReached"
        },
        "IsCountReached": {
            "Type": "Choice",
            "Choices": [
                {
                    "Variable": "$.iterator.continue",
                    "BooleanEquals": true,
                    "Next": "ExampleWork"
                }
            ],
            "Default": "ShouldRestart"
        },
        "ExampleWork": {
            "Comment": "Your application logic, to run a specific number of times",
            "Type": "Pass",
            "Result": {
              "success": true
            },
            "ResultPath": "$.result",
            "Next": "Iterator"
        },
        "ShouldRestart": {
          "Type": "Choice",
          "Choices": [
            {
              "Variable": "$.restart.executionCount",
              "NumericGreaterThan": 0,
              "Next": "Restart"
            }
          ],
          "Default": "Done"
        },
        "Restart": {
          "Type": "Task",
          "Resource": "arn:aws:lambda:us-east-1:123456789012:function:Restart",
```

```
55          "Next": "Done"
56        },
57        "Done": {
58          "Type": "Pass",
59          "End": true
60        }
61      }
62 }
```

5. Update the `Resource` string in the `Restart` and `Iterator` states to reference the respective Lambda functions you created earlier.

6. Select **Create State Machine**.

Note

Save the Amazon Resource Name of this state machine.

Step 4: Update the IAM Policy

To ensure your Lambda function has permissions to start a new Step Functions execution, attach an inline policy to the IAM role you use for your `Restart` Lambda function. For more information, see Embedding Inline Policies in the *IAM User Guide*.

```
1  {
2    "Version": "2012-10-17",
3    "Statement": [
4        {
5            "Sid": "VisualEditor0",
6            "Effect": "Allow",
7            "Action": [
8                "states:StartExecution"
9            ],
10           "Resource": "*"
11       }
12   ]
13 }
```

Note

You can update the `"Resource": "*"` line in the previous example to reference the ARN of your `ContinueAsNew` state machine. This restricts the policy so that it can only start an execution of that specific state machine.

Step 5: Run an Execution

To start an execution, provide input that includes the ARN of the state machine and an `executionCount` for how many times it should start a new execution.

1. On the **ContinueAsNew** page, choose **New execution**.

2. In the **Input** section, on the **New execution** page, enter `Test1` for the execution name. Then enter the following in the **Input**.

```
1  {
2    "restart": {
3      "StateMachineArn": "arn:aws:states:us-east-1:123456789012:stateMachine:ContinueAsNew",
4      "executionCount": 4
5    }
```

₆ }

3. Update the `StateMachineArn` field with the Amazon Resource Name for your `ContinueAsNew` state machine.

4. Choose **Start Execution**.

The **Visual Workflow** graph will display the first of the four executions. Before it completes, it will pass through the `Restart` state and start a new execution.

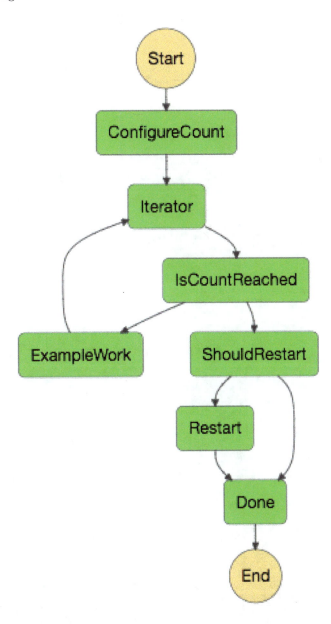

With this execution complete, you can go look at the next execution that's running. Select the **ContinueAsNew** link at the top to see the list of executions. You should see both the recently closed execution, and an ongoing execution that the `Restart` Lambda function kicked off.

Running

Once all the executions are complete, you should see four successful executions in the list. The first execution started displays the name you chose, and subsequent executions have a generated name.

8c4254e3-efa2-4b58-aa1a-fb85c8977516

arn:aws:states:us-east-1:_____:execution:ContinueAsNew:8c4254e3-efa2-4b58-a...   **Succeeded**

0c9cfbd5-bf15-470b-b675-4d6ea0934afc

arn:aws:states:us-east-1:_____:execution:ContinueAsNew:0c9cfbd5-bf15-470b-b6...   **Succeeded**

67e10aef-693a-4abb-b7e6-2805a845ddd8

arn:aws:states:us-east-1:_____:execution:ContinueAsNew:67e10aef-693a-4abb-b...   **Succeeded**

Test1

arn:aws:states:us-east-1:_____:execution:ContinueAsNew:Test1   **Succeeded**

How Step Functions Works

To understand AWS Step Functions, you will need to be familiar with a number of important concepts. This section describes how Step Functions works.

Topics

- States
- Tasks
- Activities
- Transitions
- State Machine Data
- Input and Output Processing
- Executions
- Error Handling
- Read Consistency
- Templates
- Sample Projects

States

States are top-level elements within a state machine's `States` field, and can take a number of different roles in your state machine depending on their type.

```
1  "FirstState" : {
2     "Type" : "Task",
3     ...
4  }
```

States are identified by their name, which must be unique within the state machine specification, but otherwise can be any valid string in JSON text format. Each state also contains a number of fields with options that vary according to the contents of the state's required `Type` field.

Note

State machine names must be 1–80 characters in length, must be unique for your account and region, and must not contain any of the following:

Whitespace Wildcard characters (? *) Bracket characters (< > { } [ ]) Special characters (: ; , \ | ^ ~ $ # % & "\) `Control characters` \(\u0000\-\u001for\u007f\-\u009f'). Step Functions allows you to create state machine, execution, and activity names that contain non-ASCII characters. These non-ASCII names don't work with Amazon CloudWatch. To ensure that you can track CloudWatch metrics, choose a name that uses only ASCII characters.

Topics

- Common State Fields
- Pass
- Task
- Choice
- Wait
- Succeed
- Fail
- Parallel

Tasks

All work in your state machine is done by *tasks*. A task can be an activity or a Lambda function.

- An activity consists of program code that waits for an operator to perform an action or to provide input. You can host activities on Amazon EC2, on Amazon ECS, or even on mobile devices. Activities poll Step Functions using the `GetActivityTask` and `SendTaskSuccess`, `SendTaskFailure`, and `SendTaskHeartbeat` API actions.
- A Lambda function is a cloud-native task that runs on AWS Lambda. You can write Lambda functions in a variety of programming languages, using the AWS Management Console or by uploading code to Lambda.

Amazon States Language represents tasks by setting a state's type to `Task` and by providing the task with the ARN of the activity or Lambda function. For more information about specifying task types, see Task in Amazon States Language.

To see a list of your tasks, use the **Tasks** page in the Step Functions console.

Activities

Activities are an AWS Step Functions concept that refers to a task to be performed by a *worker* that can be hosted on EC2, ECS, mobile devices—basically anywhere.

Topics

- Creating an Activity
- Writing a Worker
- Example Activity Worker in Ruby

Creating an Activity

Activities are referred to by name. An activity's name can be any string that adheres to the following rules:

- It must be between 0 – 80 characters in length.
- It must be unique within your AWS account and region.

Activities can be created with Step Functions in any of the following ways:

- Call CreateActivity with the activity name.
- Using the Step Functions console.

Note

Activities are not versioned and are expected to always be backwards compatible. If you must make a backwards-incompatible change to an activity definition, then a *new* activity should be created with Step Functions using a unique name.

Writing a Worker

Workers can be implemented in any language that can make AWS Step Functions API actions. Workers should repeatedly poll for work by implementing the following pseudo-code algorithm:

```
1  [taskToken, jsonInput] = GetActivityTask();
2  try {
3      // Do some work...
4      SendTaskSuccess(taskToken, jsonOutput);
5  } catch (Exception e) {
6      SendTaskFailure(taskToken, reason, errorCode);
7  }
```

Sending Heartbeat Notifications

States that have long-running activities should provide a heartbeat timeout value to verify that the activity is still running successfully.

If your activity has a heartbeat timeout value, the worker which implements it must send heartbeat updates to Step Functions. To send a heartbeat notification from a worker, use the SendTaskHeartbeat action.

Example Activity Worker in Ruby

The following is an example activity worker written in Ruby. This provides an implementation based on best practices that can be used as a reference for your activity worker. The code implements a consumer-producer pattern with a configurable number of threads for pollers and activity workers. The poller threads are constantly long polling the activity task. Once an activity task is retrieved, it is passed through a bounded blocking queue for the activity thread to pick it up.

- For more information on the AWS SDK for Ruby, see the AWS SDK for Ruby API Reference.
- To download this code and related resources, see step-functions-ruby-activity-worker on GitHub.com.

The following Ruby code is the main entry point and example usage for the Ruby activity worker that follows.

```ruby
require_relative '../lib/step_functions/activity'
credentials = Aws::SharedCredentials.new
region = 'us-west-2'
activity_arn = 'ACTIVITY_ARN'

activity = StepFunctions::Activity.new(
  credentials: credentials,
  region: region,
  activity_arn: activity_arn,
  workers_count: 1,
  pollers_count: 1,
  heartbeat_delay: 30
)

# The start method takes as argument the block that is the actual logic of your custom activity

activity.start do |input|
  { result: :SUCCESS, echo: input['value'] }
```

The above code includes defaults you can change to reference your activity, and to adapt it to your specific implementation. This code takes as input the actual implementation logic, allows you to reference your specific activity and credentials, and allows you to configure the number of threads and heartbeat delay. For more information and to download the code, see Step Functions Ruby Activity Worker.

Item	Description
require_relative	Relative path to the activity worker code below.
region	AWS region of your activity.
workers_count	The number of threads for your activity worker. For most implementations, between 10 and 20 threads should be sufficient. The longer the activity takes to process, the more threads it may need. As an estimate, multiply the number of process activities per second by the 99th percentile activity processing latency, in seconds.
pollers_count	The number of threads for your pollers. Between 10 and 20 threads should be sufficient for most implementations.
heartbeat_delay	The delay in seconds between heartbeats.
input	Implementation logic of your activity.

The following is the Ruby activity worker used by the example above and referenced with `../lib/step_functions/activity`.

```ruby
 1 require 'set'
 2 require 'json'
 3 require 'thread'
 4 require 'logger'
 5 require 'aws-sdk'
 6
 7 module Validate
 8   def self.positive(value)
 9     raise ArgumentError, 'Argument has to positive' if value <= 0
10     value
11   end
12
13   def self.required(value)
14     raise ArgumentError, 'Argument is required' if value.nil?
15     value
16   end
17 end
18
19 module StepFunctions
20   class RetryError < StandardError
21     def initialize(message)
22       super(message)
23     end
24   end
25
26   def self.with_retries(options = {}, &block)
27     retries = 0
28     base_delay_seconds = options[:base_delay_seconds] || 2
29     max_retries = options[:max_retries] || 3
30     begin
31       block.call
32     rescue => e
33       puts e
34       if retries < max_retries
35         retries += 1
36         sleep base_delay_seconds**retries
37         retry
38       end
39       raise RetryError, 'All retries of operation had failed'
40     end
41   end
42
43   class Activity
44     def initialize(options = {})
45       @states = Aws::States::Client.new(
46         credentials: Validate.required(options[:credentials]),
47         region: Validate.required(options[:region]),
48         http_read_timeout: Validate.positive(options[:http_read_timeout] || 60)
49       )
50       @activity_arn = Validate.required(options[:activity_arn])
51       @heartbeat_delay = Validate.positive(options[:heartbeat_delay] || 60)
52       @queue_max = Validate.positive(options[:queue_max] || 5)
```

```ruby
53      @pollers_count = Validate.positive(options[:pollers_count] || 1)
54      @workers_count = Validate.positive(options[:workers_count] || 1)
55      @max_retry = Validate.positive(options[:workers_count] || 3)
56      @logger = Logger.new(STDOUT)
57    end
58
59    def start(&block)
60      @sink = SizedQueue.new(@queue_max)
61      @activities = Set.new
62      start_heartbeat_worker(@activities)
63      start_workers(@activities, block, @sink)
64      start_pollers(@activities, @sink)
65      wait
66    end
67
68    def queue_size
69      return 0 if @sink.nil?
70      @sink.size
71    end
72
73    def activities_count
74      return 0 if @activities.nil?
75      @activities.size
76    end
77
78    private
79
80    def start_pollers(activities, sink)
81      @pollers = Array.new(@pollers_count) do
82        PollerWorker.new(
83          states: @states,
84          activity_arn: @activity_arn,
85          sink: sink,
86          activities: activities,
87          max_retry: @max_retry
88        )
89      end
90      @pollers.each(&:start)
91    end
92
93    def start_workers(activities, block, sink)
94      @workers = Array.new(@workers_count) do
95        ActivityWorker.new(
96          states: @states,
97          block: block,
98          sink: sink,
99          activities: activities,
100         max_retry: @max_retry
101        )
102      end
103      @workers.each(&:start)
104    end
105
106    def start_heartbeat_worker(activities)
```

```ruby
107        @heartbeat_worker = HeartbeatWorker.new(
108          states: @states,
109          activities: activities,
110          heartbeat_delay: @heartbeat_delay,
111          max_retry: @max_retry
112        )
113        @heartbeat_worker.start
114      end
115
116      def wait
117        sleep
118      rescue Interrupt
119        shutdown
120      ensure
121        Thread.current.exit
122      end
123
124      def shutdown
125        stop_workers(@pollers)
126        wait_workers(@pollers)
127        wait_activities_drained
128        stop_workers(@workers)
129        wait_activities_completed
130        shutdown_workers(@workers)
131        shutdown_worker(@heartbeat_worker)
132      end
133
134      def shutdown_workers(workers)
135        workers.each do |worker|
136          shutdown_worker(worker)
137        end
138      end
139
140      def shutdown_worker(worker)
141        worker.kill
142      end
143
144      def wait_workers(workers)
145        workers.each(&:wait)
146      end
147
148      def wait_activities_drained
149        wait_condition { @sink.empty? }
150      end
151
152      def wait_activities_completed
153        wait_condition { @activities.empty? }
154      end
155
156      def wait_condition(&block)
157        loop do
158          break if block.call
159          sleep(1)
160        end
```

```ruby
161    end
162
163    def stop_workers(workers)
164      workers.each(&:stop)
165    end
166
167    class Worker
168      def initialize
169        @logger = Logger.new(STDOUT)
170        @running = false
171      end
172
173      def run
174        raise 'Method run hasn\'t been implemented'
175      end
176
177      def process
178        loop do
179          begin
180            break unless @running
181            run
182          rescue => e
183            puts e
184            @logger.error('Unexpected error had occurred')
185            @logger.error(e)
186          end
187        end
188      end
189
190      def start
191        return unless @thread.nil?
192        @running = true
193        @thread = Thread.new do
194          process
195        end
196      end
197
198      def stop
199        @running = false
200      end
201
202      def kill
203        return if @thread.nil?
204        @thread.kill
205        @thread = nil
206      end
207
208      def wait
209        @thread.join
210      end
211    end
212
213    class PollerWorker < Worker
214      def initialize(options = {})
```

```ruby
215       @states = options[:states]
216       @activity_arn = options[:activity_arn]
217       @sink = options[:sink]
218       @activities = options[:activities]
219       @max_retry = options[:max_retry]
220       @logger = Logger.new(STDOUT)
221     end
222
223     def run
224       activity_task = StepFunctions.with_retries(max_retry: @max_retry) do
225         begin
226           @states.get_activity_task(activity_arn: @activity_arn)
227         rescue => e
228           @logger.error('Failed to retrieve activity task')
229           @logger.error(e)
230         end
231       end
232       return if activity_task.nil? || activity_task.task_token.nil?
233       @activities.add(activity_task.task_token)
234       @sink.push(activity_task)
235     end
236   end
237
238   class ActivityWorker < Worker
239     def initialize(options = {})
240       @states = options[:states]
241       @block = options[:block]
242       @sink = options[:sink]
243       @activities = options[:activities]
244       @max_retry = options[:max_retry]
245       @logger = Logger.new(STDOUT)
246     end
247
248     def run
249       activity_task = @sink.pop
250       result = @block.call(JSON.parse(activity_task.input))
251       send_task_success(activity_task, result)
252     rescue => e
253       send_task_failure(activity_task, e)
254     ensure
255       @activities.delete(activity_task.task_token) unless activity_task.nil?
256     end
257
258     def send_task_success(activity_task, result)
259       StepFunctions.with_retries(max_retry: @max_retry) do
260         begin
261           @states.send_task_success(
262             task_token: activity_task.task_token,
263             output: JSON.dump(result)
264           )
265         rescue => e
266           @logger.error('Failed to send task success')
267           @logger.error(e)
268         end
```

```ruby
        end
      end

      def send_task_failure(activity_task, error)
        StepFunctions.with_retries do
          begin
            @states.send_task_failure(
              task_token: activity_task.task_token,
              cause: error.message
            )
          rescue => e
            @logger.error('Failed to send task failure')
            @logger.error(e)
          end
        end
      end
    end

    class HeartbeatWorker < Worker
      def initialize(options = {})
        @states = options[:states]
        @activities = options[:activities]
        @heartbeat_delay = options[:heartbeat_delay]
        @max_retry = options[:max_retry]
        @logger = Logger.new(STDOUT)
      end

      def run
        sleep(@heartbeat_delay)
        @activities.each do |token|
          send_heartbeat(token)
        end
      end

      def send_heartbeat(token)
        StepFunctions.with_retries(max_retry: @max_retry) do
          begin
            @states.send_task_heartbeat(token)
          rescue => e
            @logger.error('Failed to send heartbeat for activity')
            @logger.error(e)
          end
        end
      rescue => e
        @logger.error('Failed to send heartbeat for activity')
        @logger.error(e)
      end
    end
  end
end
```

Transitions

When an execution of a state machine is launched, the system begins with the state referenced in the top-level `StartAt` field. This field (a string) must exactly match, including case, the name of one of the states.

After executing a state, AWS Step Functions uses the value of the `Next` field to determine the next state to advance to.

`Next` fields also specify state names as strings, and must match the name of a state specified in the state machine description exactly (case-sensitive).

For example, the following state includes a transition to `NextState`:

```
1  "SomeState" : {
2    ...,
3    "Next" : "NextState"
4  }
```

Most states permit only a single transition rule via the `Next` field. However, certain flow-control states (for example, a `Choice` state) allow you to specify multiple transition rules, each with its own `Next` field. The Amazon States Language provides details about each of the state types you can specify, including information about how to specify transitions.

States can have multiple incoming transitions from other states.

The process repeats until it reaches a terminal state (a state with `"Type"`: `Succeed`, `"Type"`: `Fail`, or `"End"`: `true`), or a runtime error occurs.

The following rules apply to states within a state machine:

- States can occur in any order within the enclosing block, but the order in which they're listed doesn't affect the order in which they're run, which is determined by the contents of the states themselves.
- Within a state machine, there can be only one state designated as the **start** state, which is designated by the value of the `StartAt` field in the top-level structure.
- Depending on your state machine logic—for example, if your state machine has multiple branches of execution—you may have more than one **end** state.
- If your state machine consists of only one state, it can be both the **start** state and the **end** state.

State Machine Data

State Machine data takes the following forms:

- The initial input into a state machine
- Data passed between states
- The output from a state machine

This section describes how state machine data is formatted and used in AWS Step Functions.

Topics

- Data Format
- State Machine Input/Output
- State Input/Output

Data Format

State machine data is represented by JSON text, so you can provide values using any data type supported by JSON:

Note

Numbers in JSON text format conform to JavaScript semantics. These numbers typically correspond to double-precision IEEE-854 values. The following is valid JSON text: stand-alone, quote-delimited strings; objects; arrays; numbers; Boolean values; and `null`. The output of a state becomes the input into the next state. However, you can restrict states to working on a subset of the input data by using Input and Output Processing.

State Machine Input/Output

You can give AWS Step Functions initial input data by passing it to a [StartExecution](http://docs.aws.amazon.com/step-functions/latest/apireference/API_StartExecution.html) action when you start an execution, or by passing initial data using the Step Functions console. Initial data is passed to the state machine's `StartAt` state. If no input is provided, the default is an empty object (`{}`).

The output of the execution is returned by the last state (`terminal`). This output appears as JSON text in the execution's result. You can retrieve execution results from the execution history using external callers (for example, in the [DescribeExecution](http://docs.aws.amazon.com/step-functions/latest/apireference/API_DescribeExecution.html) action). You can view execution results on the Step Functions console.

State Input/Output

Each state's input consists of JSON text from the preceding state or, for the `StartAt` state, the input into the execution. Certain flow-control states echo their input to their output.

In the following example, the state machine adds two numbers together:

1. Define the Lambda function.

```
1 function Add(input) {
2   var numbers = JSON.parse(input).numbers;
3   var total = numbers.reduce(
4     function(previousValue, currentValue, index, array) {
5       return previousValue + currentValue; });
6   return JSON.stringify({ result: total });
7 }
```

2. Define the state machine.

```
1  {
2    "Comment": "An example that adds two numbers together.",
3    "StartAt": "Add",
4    "Version": "1.0",
5    "TimeoutSeconds": 10,
6    "States":
7      {
8          "Add": {
9            "Type": "Task",
10           "Resource": "arn:aws:lambda:us-east-1:123456789012:function:Add",
11           "End": true
12         }
13      }
14 }
```

3. Start an execution with the following JSON text:

```
1  { "numbers": [3, 4] }
```

The **Add** state receives the JSON text and passes it to the Lambda function

The Lambda function returns the result of the calculation to the state.

The state returns the following value in its output:

```
1  { "result": 7 }
```

Because **Add** is also the final state in the state machine, this value is returned as the state machine's output.

If the final state returns no output, then the state machine returns an empty object ({}).

For more information, see Input and Output Processing in Step Functions

Input and Output Processing in Step Functions

A Step Functions execution receives a JSON file as input and passes that input to the first state in the workflow. Individual states receive JSON as input and usually pass JSON as output to the next state. Understanding how this information flows from state to state, and learning how to filter and manipulate this data, is key to effectively designing and implementing workflows in AWS Step Functions.

In the Amazon States Language, three components filter and control the flow of JSON from state to state:

- InputPath
- OutputPath
- ResultPath

The following diagram shows how JSON information moves through a task state. InputPath selects which components from the input to pass to the task of the Task state (for example, an AWS Lambda function). ResultPath then selects what combination of the state input and the task result to pass to the output. OutputPath can filter the JSON output to further limit the information that is passed to the output.

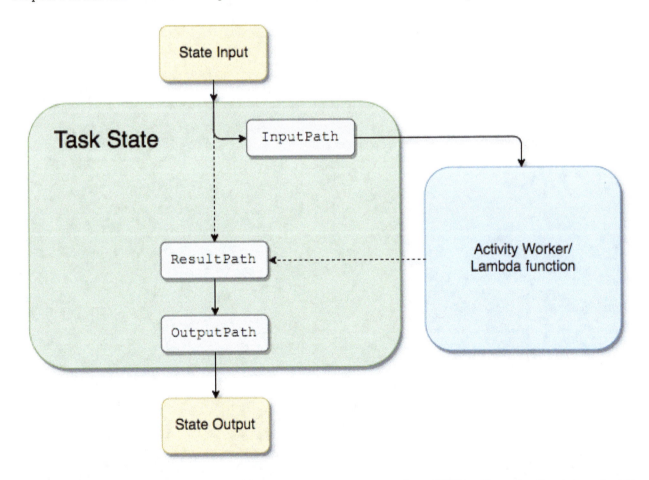

InputPath, OutputPath, and ResultPath each use paths to manipulate JSON as it moves through each state in your workflow. A path is a string, beginning with $, that identifies components within JSON text. Step Functions paths use JsonPath syntax.

Note
ResultPath is limited to using reference paths, which limit scope so that it can identify only a single node in JSON. See Reference Paths in the Amazon States Language.

Topics

- Understanding `ResultPath`
- Filtering with `InputPath` and `OutputPath`

Understanding `ResultPath`

The output of a state can be a copy of its input, the result it produces (for example, output from a Task state's Lambda function), or a combination of its input and result. Use`ResultPath` to control which combination of these is passed to the state output.

The following state types can generate a result and can include `ResultPath`:

- Pass
- Task
- Parallel

Use `ResultPath` to combine a task result with task input, or to select one of these. The path you provide to `ResultPath`controls what information passes to the output.

These examples are based on the state machine and Lambda function described in the Creating a Lambda State Machine tutorial. Work through that tutorial and test different outputs by trying various paths in a `ResultPath` field.

Use `ResultPath` to:

- Replace Input With Result
- Include Result With Input
- Update a Node in Input With Result
- Include Error and Input in a `Catch`

Use `ResultPath` to Replace Input with Result

If you don't specify a `ResultPath`, the default behavior is as if you had specified `"ResultPath"`: `"$"`. Because this tells the state to replace the entire input with the result, the state input is completely replaced by the result coming from the task result.

The following diagram shows how `ResultPath` can completely replace the input with the result of the task.

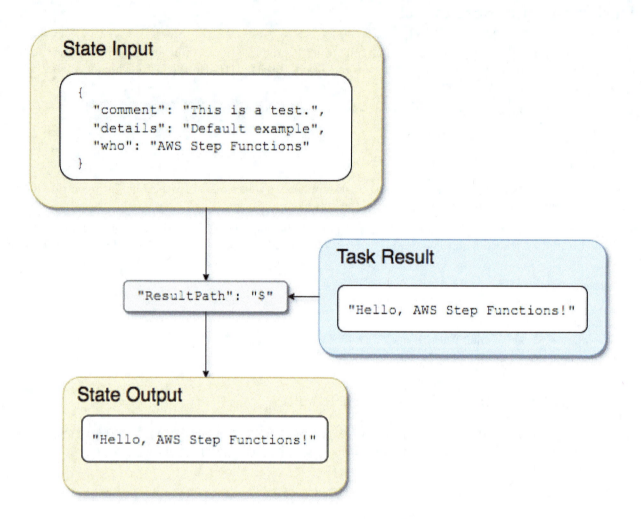

Using the state machine and Lambda function described in Creating a Lambda State Machine, if we pass the following input:

```
1 {
2   "comment": "This is a test of the input and output of a Task state.",
3   "details": "Default example",
4   "who": "AWS Step Functions"
5 }
```

The Lambda function provides the following result:

```
1 "Hello, AWS Step Functions!"
```

If ResultPath isn't specified in the state, or if "ResultPath": "$" is set, the input of the state is replaced by the result of the Lambda function, and the output of the state is:

```
1 "Hello, AWS Step Functions!"
```

Note
ResultPath is used to include content from the result with the input, before passing it to the output. But, if ResultPath isn't specified, the default is to replace the entire input.

Use `ResultPath` to Include Result with Input

The following diagram shows how `ResultPath` can include the result with the input.

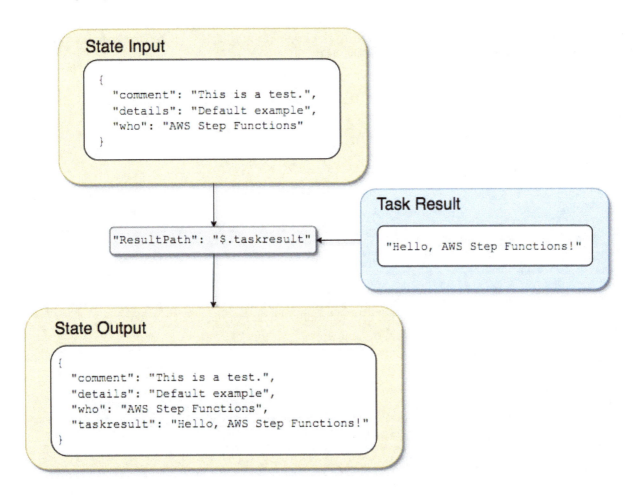

Using the state machine and Lambda function described in the Creating a Lambda State Machine tutorial, we could pass the following input:

```
1 {
2   "comment": "This is a test of the input and output of a Task state.",
3   "details": "Default example",
4   "who": "AWS Step Functions"
5 }
```

The result of the Lambda function is:

```
1 "Hello, AWS Step Functions!"
```

If we want to preserve the input, insert the result of the Lambda function, and then pass the combined JSON to the next state, we could set `ResultPath` to:

```
1 "ResultPath": "$.taskresult"
```

This includes the result of the Lambda function with the original input:

```
1 {
2   "comment": "This is a test of input and output of a Task state.",
```

```
3    "details": "Default behavior example",
4    "who": "AWS Step Functions",
5    "taskresult": "Hello, AWS Step Functions!"
6  }
```

The output of the Lambda function is appended to the original input as a value for `taskresult`. The input, including the newly inserted value, is passed to the next state.

You can also insert the result into a child node of the input. Set the `ResultPath` to:

```
1  "ResultPath": "$.strings.lambdaresult"
```

Start an execution using the following input:

```
1  {
2    "comment": "An input comment.",
3    "strings": {
4      "string1": "foo",
5      "string2": "bar",
6      "string3": "baz"
7    },
8    "who": "AWS Step Functions"
9  }
```

The result of the Lambda function is inserted as a child of the `strings` node in the input:

```
1  {
2    "comment": "An input comment.",
3    "strings": {
4      "string1": "foo",
5      "string2": "bar",
6      "string3": "baz",
7      "lambdaresult": "Hello, AWS Step Functions!"
8    },
9    "who": "AWS Step Functions"
10 }
```

The state output now includes the original input JSON with the result as a child node.

Use ResultPath to Update a Node in Input with the Result

The following diagram shows how `ResultPath` can update the value of existing JSON nodes in the input with values from the task result.

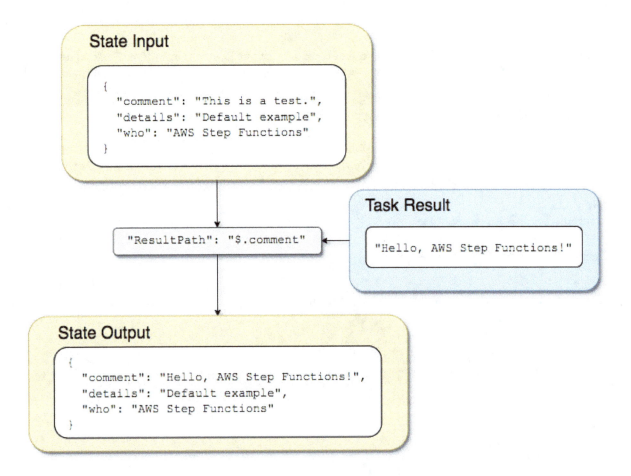

Using the example of the state machine and Lambda function described in the Creating a Lambda State Machine tutorial, we could pass the following input:

```
1 {
2   "comment": "This is a test of the input and output of a Task state.",
3   "details": "Default example",
4   "who": "AWS Step Functions"
5 }
```

The result of the Lambda function is:

```
1 Hello, AWS Step Functions!
```

Instead of preserving the input and inserting the result as a new node in the JSON, we can overwrite an existing node. For example, just as omitting or setting `"ResultPath": "$"` overwrites the entire node, you can specify an individual node to overwrite with the result:

```
1 "ResultPath": "$.comment"
```

Because the `comment` node already exists in the state input, setting `ResultPath` to `"$.comment"` replaces that node in the input with the result of the Lambda function. Without further filtering by `OutputPath`, the following is passed to the output:

```
1 {
2   "comment": "Hello, AWS Step Functions!",
3   "details": "Default behavior example",
```

```
4    "who": "AWS Step Functions",
5  }
```

The value for the `comment` node, `"This is a test of the input and output of a Task state."`, is replaced by the result of the Lambda function: `"Hello, AWS Step Functions!"` in the state output.

Use `ResultPath` to Include Both Error and Input in a `Catch`

The Handling Error Conditions Using a State Machine tutorial shows how to use a state machine to catch an error. In some cases, you might want to preserve the original input with the error. Use `ResultPath` in a `Catch` to include the error with the original input, rather than replace it:

```
1  "Catch": [{
2    "ErrorEquals": ["States.ALL"],
3    "Next": "NextTask",
4    "ResultPath": "$.error"
5  }]
```

If the previous `Catch` statement catches an error, it includes the result in an `error` node within the state input. For example, with the following input:

```
1  {"foo": "bar"}
```

The state output when catching an error is:

```
1  {
2    "foo": "bar",
3    "error": {
4      "Error": "Error here"
5    }
6  }
```

For more information about error handling, see:

- Error Handling
- Handling Error Conditions Using a State Machine

Filtering with InputPath and OutputPath

Any state other than a `Fail` state can include `InputPath` or `OutputPath`. These allow you to use a path to filter the JSON as it moves through your workflow.

For example, start with the AWS Lambda function and state machine described in the Creating a Lambda State Machine tutorial. Modify the state machine so that it includes the following `InputPath`, `ResultPath`, and `OutputPath`:

```
1  {
2    "Comment": "A Hello World example of the Amazon States Language using an AWS Lambda function",
3    "StartAt": "HelloWorld",
4    "States": {
5      "HelloWorld": {
6        "Type": "Task",
7        "Resource": "arn:aws:lambda:us-east-1:123456789012:function:HelloFunction",
8        "InputPath": "$.lambda",
9        "ResultPath": "$.data.lambdaresult",
10       "OutputPath": "$.data",
11       "End": true
12     }
13   }
14 }
```

Start an execution using the following input:

```
1  {
2    "comment": "An input comment.",
3    "data": {
4      "val1": 23,
5      "val2": 17
6    },
7    "extra": "foo",
8    "lambda": {
9      "who": "AWS Step Functions"
10   }
11 }
```

Assume that the `comment` and `extra` nodes can be discarded, but that we want to include the output of the Lambda function, as well as preserve the information in the `data` node.

In the updated state machine, the `Task` state is altered to process the input to the task:

```
1  "InputPath": "$.lambda",
```

This line in the state machine definition limits the task input to only the `lambda` node from the state input. The Lambda function receives only the JSON object `{"who": "AWS Step Functions"}` as input.

```
1  "ResultPath": "$.data.lambdaresult",
```

This `ResultPath` tells the state machine to insert the result of the Lambda function into a node named `lambdaresult`, as a child of the `data` node in the original state machine input. Without further processing with `OutputPath`, the input of the state now includes the result of the Lambda function with the original input:

```
1  {
2    "comment": "An input comment.",
3    "data": {
4      "val1": 23,
```

```
5      "val2": 17,
6      "lambdaresult": "Hello, AWS Step Functions!"
7    },
8    "extra": "foo",
9    "lambda": {
10      "who": "AWS Step Functions"
11    }
12 }
```

But, our goal was to preserve only the **data** node, and include the result of the Lambda function. `OutputPath` filters this combined JSON before passing it to the state output:

```
1 "OutputPath": "$.data",
```

This selects only the **data** node from the original input (including the `lambdaresult` child inserted by `ResultPath`) to be passed to the output. The state output is filtered to:

```
1 {
2    "val1": 23,
3    "val2": 17,
4    "lambdaresult": "Hello, AWS Step Functions!"
5 }
```

In this Task state:

1. `InputPath` sends only the `lambda` node from the input to the Lambda function.

2. `ResultPath` inserts the result as a child of the **data** node in the original input.

3. `OutputPath` filters the state input (which now includes the result of the Lambda function) so that it passes only the **data** node to the state output.

For more information, see: Input and Output Processing in Step Functions.

Executions

A state machine *execution* occurs when a Step Functions state machine runs and performs its tasks. Each Step Functions state machine can have multiple simultaneous executions which you can initiate from the Step Functions console, or using the AWS SDKs, the Step Functions API actions, or the AWS CLI. An execution receives JSON input and produces JSON output.

For more information about the different ways of working with Step Functions, see Development Options. For more information about initiating an execution from the Step Functions console, see To start a new execution.

Note
The Step Functions console displays a maximum of 1,000 executions per state machine. If you have more than 1,000 executions, use the Step Functions API actions, or the AWS CLI to display all of your executions.

Error Handling

Any state can encounter runtime errors. Errors can happen for various reasons:

- State machine definition issues (for example, no matching rule in a `Choice` state).
- Task failures (for example, an exception in a Lambda function).
- Transient issues (for example, network partition events).

By default, when a state reports an error, Step Functions causes the execution to fail entirely.

Error Names

Step Functions identifies errors in Amazon States Language using case-sensitive strings, known as *error names*. Amazon States Language defines a set of built-in strings that name well-known errors, all beginning with the `States.` prefix.

** `States.ALL` **
A wildcard that matches any known error name.

** `States.Timeout` **
A `Task` state either ran longer than the `TimeoutSeconds` value, or failed to send a heartbeat for a period longer than the `HeartbeatSeconds` value.

** `States.TaskFailed` **
A `Task` state failed during the execution.

** `States.Permissions` **
A `Task` state failed because it had insufficient privileges to execute the specified code.

States can report errors with other names. However, these must not begin with the `States.` prefix.

Note
Unhandled errors in Lambda are reported as `Lambda.Unknown` in the error output. These include out-of-memory errors, function timeouts, and hitting the concurrent Lambda invoke limit. You can match on `Lambda.Unknown`, `States.ALL`, or `States.TaskFailed` to handle these errors. For more information about Lambda `Handled` and `Unhandled` errors, see `FunctionError` in the AWS Lambda Developer Guide.

Retrying After an Error

`Task` and `Parallel` states can have a field named `Retry`, whose value must be an array of objects known as *retriers*. An individual retrier represents a certain number of retries, usually at increasing time intervals.

Note
Retries are treated as state transitions. For information on how state transitions affect billing, see Step Functions Pricing.

A retrier contains the following fields:

** `ErrorEquals` (Required)**
A non-empty array of strings that match error names. When a state reports an error, Step Functions scans through the retriers. When the error name appears in this array, it implements the retry policy described in this retrier.

** `IntervalSeconds` (Optional)**
An integer that represents the number of seconds before the first retry attempt (1 by default).

** `MaxAttempts` (Optional)**
A positive integer that represents the maximum number of retry attempts (3 by default). If the error recurs

more times than specified, retries cease and normal error handling resumes. A value of 0 specifies that the error or errors are never retried.

** `BackoffRate` (Optional)**

The multiplier by which the retry interval increases during each attempt (2.0 by default).

This example of a `Retry` makes 2 retry attempts after waiting for 3 and 4.5 seconds.

```
1  "Retry": [ {
2      "ErrorEquals": [ "States.Timeout" ],
3      "IntervalSeconds": 3,
4      "MaxAttempts": 2,
5      "BackoffRate": 1.5
6  } ]
```

The reserved name `States.ALL` that appears in a Retrier's `ErrorEquals` field is a wildcard that matches any error name. It must appear alone in the `ErrorEquals` array and must appear in the last retrier in the `Retry` array.

This example of a `Retry` field retries any error except `States.Timeout`.

```
1  "Retry": [ {
2      "ErrorEquals": [ "States.Timeout" ],
3      "MaxAttempts": 0
4  }, {
5      "ErrorEquals": [ "States.ALL" ]
6  } ]
```

Complex Retry Scenarios

A retrier's parameters apply across all visits to the retrier in the context of a single-state execution. Consider the following **Task** state:

```
1  "X": {
2      "Type": "Task",
3      "Resource": "arn:aws:states:us-east-1:123456789012:task:X",
4      "Next": "Y",
5      "Retry": [ {
6          "ErrorEquals": [ "ErrorA", "ErrorB" ],
7          "IntervalSeconds": 1,
8          "BackoffRate": 2.0,
9          "MaxAttempts": 2
10     }, {
11         "ErrorEquals": [ "ErrorC" ],
12         "IntervalSeconds": 5
13     } ],
14     "Catch": [ {
15         "ErrorEquals": [ "States.ALL" ],
16         "Next": "Z"
17     } ]
18 }
```

This task fails five times in succession, outputting these error names: `ErrorA`, `ErrorB`, `ErrorC`, `ErrorB`, and `ErrorB`. The following occurs as a result:

- The first two errors match the first retrier and cause waits of 1 and 2 seconds.
- The third error matches the second retrier and causes a wait of 5 seconds.

- The fourth error matches the first retrier and causes a wait of 4 seconds.
- The fifth error also matches the first retrier. However, it has already reached its limit of two retries (`MaxAttempts`) for that particular error (`ErrorB`), so it fails and execution is redirected to the `Z` state via the `Catch` field.

Fallback States

`Task` and `Parallel` states can have a field named `Catch`. This field's value must be an array of objects, known as *catchers*.

A catcher contains the following fields:

** `ErrorEquals` (Required)**
A non-empty array of Strings that match error names, specified exactly as they are with the retrier field of the same name.

** `Next` (Required)**
A string that must exactly match one of the state machine's state names.

** `ResultPath` (Optional)**
A path that determines what input is sent to the state specified in the `Next` field.

When a state reports an error and either there is no `Retry` field, or if retries fail to resolve the error, Step Functions scans through the catchers in the order listed in the array. When the error name appears in the value of a catcher's `ErrorEquals` field, the state machine transitions to the state named in the `Next` field.

The reserved name `States.ALL` that appears in a catcher's `ErrorEquals` field is a wildcard that matches any error name. It must appear alone in the `ErrorEquals` array and must appear in the last catcher in the `Catch` array.

The following example of a `Catch` field transitions to the state named `RecoveryState` when a Lambda function outputs an unhandled Java exception. Otherwise, the field transitions to the `EndState` state:

```
1 "Catch": [ {
2   "ErrorEquals": [ "java.lang.Exception" ],
3   "ResultPath": "$.error-info",
4   "Next": "RecoveryState"
5 }, {
6   "ErrorEquals": [ "States.ALL" ],
7   "Next": "EndState"
8 } ]
```

Note
Each catcher can specify multiple errors to handle.

Error Output

When Step Functions transitions to the state specified in a catch name, the object usually contains the field `Cause`. This field's value is a human-readable description of the error. This object is known as the *error output*.

In this example, the first catcher contains a `ResultPath` field. This works similarly to a `ResultPath` field in a state's top level, resulting in two possibilities:

- It takes the results of executing the state and overwrites a portion of the state's input (or all of the state's input).
- It takes the results and adds them to the input. In the case of an error handled by a catcher, the result of executing the state is the error output.

Thus, in this example, for the first catcher the error output is added to the input as a field named `error-info` (if there isn't already a field with this name in the input). Then, the entire input is sent to `RecoveryState`. For the second catcher, the error output overwrites the input and only the error output is sent to `EndState`.

Note
If you don't specify the `ResultPath` field, it defaults to $, which selects and overwrites the entire input.

When a state has both `Retry` and `Catch` fields, Step Functions uses any appropriate retriers first, and only afterward applies the matching catcher transition if the retry policy fails to resolve the error.

Examples Using Retry and Using Catch

The state machines defined in the following examples assume the existence of two Lambda functions: one that always fails and one that waits long enough to allow a timeout defined in the state machine to occur.

This is a definition of a Lambda function that always fails, returning the message **error**. In the state machine examples that follow, this Lambda function is named `FailFunction`.

```
1  exports.handler = (event, context, callback) => {
2      callback("error");
3  };
```

This is a definition of a Lambda function that sleeps for 10 seconds. In the state machine examples that follow, this Lambda function is named `sleep10`.

Note
When you create this Lambda function in the Lambda console, remember to change the **Timeout** value in the **Advanced settings** section from 3 seconds (default) to 11 seconds.

```
1  exports.handler = (event, context, callback) => {
2      setTimeout(function(){
3      }, 11000);
4  };
```

Handling a Failure Using Retry

This state machine uses a `Retry` field to retry a function that fails and outputs the error name `HandledError`. The function is retried twice with an exponential backoff between retries.

```
1  {
2      "Comment": "A Hello World example of the Amazon States Language using an AWS Lambda function
          ",
3      "StartAt": "HelloWorld",
4      "States": {
5          "HelloWorld": {
6              "Type": "Task",
7              "Resource": "arn:aws:lambda:us-east-1:123456789012:function:FailFunction",
8              "Retry": [ {
9                  "ErrorEquals": ["HandledError"],
10                 "IntervalSeconds": 1,
11                 "MaxAttempts": 2,
12                 "BackoffRate": 2.0
13             } ],
14         "End": true
15         }
16     }
17 }
```

This variant uses the predefined error code `States.TaskFailed`, which matches any error that a Lambda function outputs.

```
1  {
2      "Comment": "A Hello World example of the Amazon States Language using an AWS Lambda function
           ",
3      "StartAt": "HelloWorld",
4      "States": {
5        "HelloWorld": {
6          "Type": "Task",
7          "Resource": "arn:aws:lambda:us-east-1:123456789012:function:FailFunction",
8          "Retry": [ {
9            "ErrorEquals": ["States.TaskFailed"],
10           "IntervalSeconds": 1,
11           "MaxAttempts": 2,
12           "BackoffRate": 2.0
13         } ],
14         "End": true
15       }
16     }
17  }
```

Handling a Failure Using Catch

This example uses a `Catch` field. When a Lambda function outputs an error, the error is caught and the state machine transitions to the `fallback` state.

```
1  {
2      "Comment": "A Hello World example of the Amazon States Language using an AWS Lambda function
           ",
3      "StartAt": "HelloWorld",
4      "States": {
5        "HelloWorld": {
6          "Type": "Task",
7          "Resource": "arn:aws:lambda:us-east-1:123456789012:function:FailFunction",
8          "Catch": [ {
9            "ErrorEquals": ["HandledError"],
10           "Next": "fallback"
11         } ],
12         "End": true
13       },
14       "fallback": {
15         "Type": "Pass",
16         "Result": "Hello, AWS Step Functions!",
17         "End": true
18       }
19     }
20  }
```

This variant uses the predefined error code `States.TaskFailed`, which matches any error that a Lambda function outputs.

```
1  {
2      "Comment": "A Hello World example of the Amazon States Language using an AWS Lambda function
           ",
```

```
3    "StartAt": "HelloWorld",
4    "States": {
5      "HelloWorld": {
6        "Type": "Task",
7        "Resource": "arn:aws:lambda:us-east-1:123456789012:function:FailFunction",
8        "Catch": [ {
9          "ErrorEquals": ["States.TaskFailed"],
10         "Next": "fallback"
11       } ],
12       "End": true
13     },
14     "fallback": {
15       "Type": "Pass",
16       "Result": "Hello, AWS Step Functions!",
17       "End": true
18     }
19   }
20 }
```

Handling a Timeout Using Retry

This state machine uses a `Retry` field to retry a function that times out. The function is retried twice with an exponential backoff between retries.

```
1  {
2    "Comment": "A Hello World example of the Amazon States Language using an AWS Lambda function
       ",
3    "StartAt": "HelloWorld",
4    "States": {
5      "HelloWorld": {
6        "Type": "Task",
7        "Resource": "arn:aws:lambda:us-east-1:123456789012:function:sleep10",
8        "TimeoutSeconds": 2,
9        "Retry": [ {
10         "ErrorEquals": ["States.Timeout"],
11         "IntervalSeconds": 1,
12         "MaxAttempts": 2,
13         "BackoffRate": 2.0
14       } ],
15       "End": true
16     }
17   }
18 }
```

Handling a Timeout Using Catch

This example uses a `Catch` field. When a timeout occurs, the state machine transitions to the `fallback` state.

```
1  {
2    "Comment": "A Hello World example of the Amazon States Language using an AWS Lambda function
       ",
3    "StartAt": "HelloWorld",
4    "States": {
```

```
 5        "HelloWorld": {
 6            "Type": "Task",
 7            "Resource": "arn:aws:lambda:us-east-1:123456789012:function:sleep10",
 8            "TimeoutSeconds": 2,
 9            "Catch": [ {
10                "ErrorEquals": ["States.Timeout"],
11                "Next": "fallback"
12            } ],
13            "End": true
14        },
15        "fallback": {
16            "Type": "Pass",
17            "Result": "Hello, AWS Step Functions!",
18            "End": true
19        }
20    }
21 }
```

Note

You can preserve the state input along with the error by using `ResultPath`. See Use `ResultPath` to Include Both Error and Input in a `Catch`

Read Consistency

State machine updates in AWS Step Functions are eventually consistent. All `StartExecution` calls within a few seconds will use the updated definition and `roleArn` (the Amazon Resource Name for the IAM role). Executions started immediately after calling `UpdateStateMachine` might use the previous state machine definition and `roleArn`.

For more information, see:

- http://docs.aws.amazon.com/step-functions/latest/apireference/API_UpdateStateMachine.html — in the AWS Step Functions API Reference
- Step 3: (Optional) Update a State Machine — in the Getting Started section

Templates

In the Step Functions console, you can choose one of the following state machine templates to automatically fill the **Code** pane. Each of the templates is fully functional and you can use any blueprint as the template for your own state machine.

Note
Choosing any of the templates overwrites the contents of the **Code** pane.

- **Hello world** – A state machine with a `Pass` state.
- **Wait state** – A state machine that demonstrates different ways of injecting a `Wait` state into a running state machine:
  - By waiting for a number of seconds.
  - By waiting for an absolute time (timestamp).
  - By specifying the `Wait` state's definition.
  - By using the state's input data.
- **Retry failure** – A state machine that retries a task after the task fails. This blueprint demonstrates how to handle multiple retries and various failure types.
- **Parallel** – A state machine that demonstrates how to execute two branches at the same time.
- **Catch failure** – A state machine that performs a different task after its primary task fails. This blueprint demonstrates how to call different tasks depending on the failure type.
- **Choice state** – A state machine that makes a choice: It either runs a `Task` state from a set of `Task` states or runs a `Fail` state after the initial state is complete.

Sample Projects

In the Step Functions console, you can choose one of the following state machine sample projects to automatically create the state machine **Code**, **Visual Workflow**, and all related AWS resources for the project. Each of the sample projects provisions a fully functional state machine, and creates the related resources for it to run. When you create a sample project, Step Functions uses AWS CloudFormation to create the related resources referenced by the state machine.

Topics

- Job Status Poller
- Task Timer

Job Status Poller

This sample project creates an AWS Batch job status poller. It implements an AWS Step Functions state machine that uses AWS Lambda to create a `Wait` state loop that checks on an AWS Batch job. This sample project creates and configures all resources so that your Step Functions workflow will submit an AWS Batch job, and will wait for that job to complete before ending successfully.

This sample project creates the state machine, two Lambda functions, an AWS Batch queue, and configures the related IAM permissions. For more information on the resources that are created with the **Job Status Poller** sample project, see:

- AWS CloudFormation User Guide
- AWS Batch User Guide
- AWS Lambda Developer Guide
- IAM Getting Started Guide

To create the **Job Status Poller** state machine and provision all resources:

1. Log in to the Step Functions console, and choose **Create a state machine**.

2. Select **Sample Projects** and choose **Job Status Poller**.

   The state machine **Code** and **Visual Workflow** are displayed.

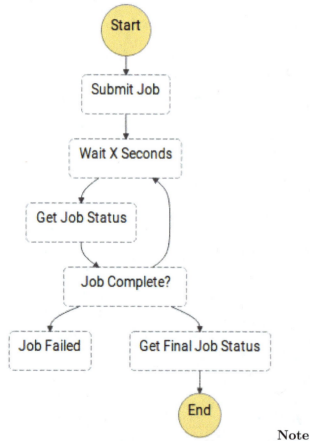

   Note

   The **Code** section in this state machine references the AWS resources that will be created for this sample project.

3. Choose **Create Sample Project**.

   The **Create Project Resources** window is displayed, listing the resources that will be created. For this sample project the resources include:

- A SubmitJob Lambda function
- A CheckJob Lambda function
- A SampleJobQueue Batch Job Queue **Note**
  It can take up to 10 minutes as these resources and related IAM permissions are created. While the **Create Project Resources** window displays **Creating resources**, you can open the **Stack ID** link to see which resources are being provisioned.

Once complete, the **New execution** window is displayed, with example input similar to this:

```
1 {
2    "jobName": "my-job",
3    "jobDefinition": "arn:aws:batch:us-east-2:123456789012:job-definition/SampleJobDefinition
        -343f54b445d5312:1",
4    "jobQueue": "arn:aws:batch:us-east-2:123456789012:job-queue/SampleJobQueue-4
        d9d696031e1449",
5    "wait_time": 60
6 }
```

Starting an Execution

After you create your state machine, you can start an execution.

To start a new execution

1. On the **New execution** page, enter an execution name (optional) and choose **Start Execution.**

2. (Optional) To help identify your execution, you can specify an ID for it in the **Enter an execution name** box. If you don't enter an ID, Step Functions generates a unique ID automatically. **Note**
   Step Functions allows you to create state machine, execution, and activity names that contain non-ASCII characters. These non-ASCII names don't work with Amazon CloudWatch. To ensure that you can track CloudWatch metrics, choose a name that uses only ASCII characters.

3. Optionally, you can go to the newly-created state machine on the Step Functions **Dashboard**, select **New execution**, and enter the input code using the names or Amazon Resource Names of your newly created resources.

   For instance, the input for the above execution using only the resource names would be:

```
1 {
2    "jobName": "my-job",
3    "jobDefinition": "SampleJobDefinition-343f54b445d5312",
4    "jobQueue": "SampleJobQueue-4d9d696031e1449",
5    "wait_time": 60
6 }
```

Note
wait_time instructs the Wait state to loop every sixty seconds.

1. Choose **Start Execution.**

   A new execution of your state machine starts, and a new page showing your running execution is displayed.

2. (Optional) In the **Execution Details** section, choose **Info** to view the **Execution Status** and the **Started** and **Closed** timestamps.

3. To view the changing status of your AWS Batch job and the looping results of your execution, choose **Output**.

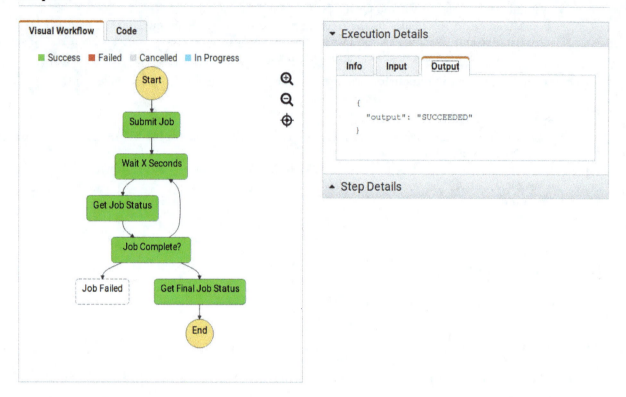

Task Timer

This sample project creates a task timer. It implements an AWS Step Functions state machine that implements a wait state, and uses a Lambda function to that sends an Amazon Simple Notification Service notification. A Wait state is a state type that waits for a trigger to perform a single unit of work.

This sample project creates the state machine, a Lambda function, an Amazon SNS topic, and configures the related IAM permissions. For more information on the resources that are created with the **Task Timer** sample project, see:

- AWS CloudFormation User Guide
- Amazon Simple Notification Service Developer Guide
- AWS Lambda Developer Guide
- IAM Getting Started Guide

To create the **Task Timer** state machine and provision all resources:

1. Log in to the Step Functions console, and choose **Create a state machine**.

2. Select **Sample Projects** and choose **Task Timer**.

   The state machine **Code** and **Visual Workflow** are displayed.

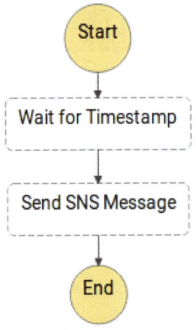

Note

The **Code** section in this state machine references the AWS resources that will be created for this sample project.

3. Choose **Create Sample Project**.

   The **Create Project Resources** window is displayed, listing the resources that will be created. For this sample project the resources include:

   - A SendToSNS Lambda function
   - A TaskTimerTopic Amazon SNS topic **Note**
     It can take up to 10 minutes as these resources and related IAM permissions are created. While the **Create Project Resources** window displays **Creating resources**, you can open the **Stack ID:** link to see which resources are being provisioned.

   Once complete, the **New execution** window is displayed, with example input similar to this:

101

```
1 {
2   "topic": "arn:aws:sns:us-east-2:123456789012:StepFunctionsSample-TaskTimer-517b8680-e0ad
        -07cf-feee-65aa5fc63ac0-SNSTopic-96RHT77RAKTS",
3   "message": "HelloWorld",
4   "timer_seconds": 10
5 }
```

4. Choose **Start Execution**.

   A new execution of your state machine starts, and a new page showing your running execution is displayed.

5. (Optional) In the **Execution Details** section, choose **Info** to view the **Execution Status** and the **Started** and **Closed** timestamps.

6. To view the changing status of your AWS Batch job and the looping results of your execution, choose **Output**.

Amazon States Language

Amazon States Language is a JSON-based, structured language used to define your state machine, a collection of states, that can do work (`Task` states), determine which states to transition to next (`Choice` states), stop an execution with an error (`Fail` states), and so on. For more information, see the Amazon States Language Specification and Statelint, a tool that validates Amazon States Language code.

To create a state machine on the Step Functions console using Amazon States Language, see Getting Started.

Topics

- Example Amazon States Language Specification
- State Machine Structure
- States
- Input and Output Processing
- Errors

Example Amazon States Language Specification

```
1  {
2    "Comment": "An example of the Amazon States Language using a choice state.",
3    "StartAt": "FirstState",
4    "States": {
5      "FirstState": {
6        "Type": "Task",
7        "Resource": "arn:aws:lambda:us-east-1:123456789012:function:FUNCTION_NAME",
8        "Next": "ChoiceState"
9      },
10     "ChoiceState": {
11       "Type" : "Choice",
12       "Choices": [
13         {
14           "Variable": "$.foo",
15           "NumericEquals": 1,
16           "Next": "FirstMatchState"
17         },
18         {
19           "Variable": "$.foo",
20           "NumericEquals": 2,
21           "Next": "SecondMatchState"
22         }
23       ],
24       "Default": "DefaultState"
25     },
26
27     "FirstMatchState": {
28       "Type" : "Task",
29       "Resource": "arn:aws:lambda:us-east-1:123456789012:function:OnFirstMatch",
30       "Next": "NextState"
31     },
32
33     "SecondMatchState": {
34       "Type" : "Task",
35       "Resource": "arn:aws:lambda:us-east-1:123456789012:function:OnSecondMatch",
```

```
36        "Next": "NextState"
37      },
38
39      "DefaultState": {
40        "Type": "Fail",
41        "Error": "DefaultStateError",
42        "Cause": "No Matches!"
43      },
44
45      "NextState": {
46        "Type": "Task",
47        "Resource": "arn:aws:lambda:us-east-1:123456789012:function:FUNCTION_NAME",
48        "End": true
49      }
50    }
51 }
```

State Machine Structure

State machines are defined using JSON text that represents a structure containing the following fields:

** Comment (Optional)**
A human-readable description of the state machine.

** StartAt (Required)**
A string that must exactly match (case-sensitive) the name of one of the state objects.

** TimeoutSeconds (Optional)**
The maximum number of seconds an execution of the state machine may run; if it runs longer than the specified time, then the execution fails with an States.Timeout Error name.

** Version (Optional)**
The version of Amazon States Language used in the state machine, default is "1.0".

** States (Required)**
This field's value is an object containing a comma-delimited set of states.

The States field contains a number of States:

```
1 {
2     "State1" : {
3     },
4
5     "State2" : {
6     },
7     ...
8 }
```

A state machine is defined by the states it contains and the relationships between them.

Here's an example:

```
1 {
2   "Comment": "A Hello World example of the Amazon States Language using a Pass state",
3   "StartAt": "HelloWorld",
4   "States": {
5     "HelloWorld": {
6       "Type": "Pass",
```

```
 7        "Result": "Hello World!",
 8        "End": true
 9      }
10    }
11 }
```

When an execution of this state machine is launched, the system begins with the state referenced in the `StartAt` field (`"HelloWorld"`). If this state has an `"End"`: `true` field, the execution stops and returns a result. Otherwise, the system looks for a `"Next"`: field and continues with that state next. This process repeats until the system reaches a terminal state (a state with `"Type"`: `"Succeed"`, `"Type"`: `"Fail"`, or `"End"`: `true`), or a runtime error occurs.

The following rules apply to states within a state machine:

- States can occur in any order within the enclosing block, but the order in which they're listed doesn't affect the order in which they're run, which is determined by the contents of the states themselves.
- Within a state machine, there can be only one state that's designated as the **start** state, designated by the value of the `StartAt` field in the top-level structure. This state is the one that is executed first when the execution starts.
- Any state for which the `End` field is `true` is considered to be an **end** (or **terminal**) state. Depending on your state machine logic—for example, if your state machine has multiple branches of execution—you may have more than one **end** state.
- If your state machine consists of only one state, it can be both the **start** state and the **end** state.

Common State Fields

** Type (Required)**
The state's type.

** Next **
The name of the next state that will be run when the current state finishes. Some state types, such as **Choice**, allow multiple transition states.

** End **
Designates this state as a terminal state (it ends the execution) if set to **true**. There can be any number of terminal states per state machine. Only one of **Next** or **End** can be used in a state. Some state types, such as **Choice**, do not support or use the **End** field.

** Comment (Optional)**
Holds a human-readable description of the state.

** InputPath (Optional)**
A path that selects a portion of the state's input to be passed to the state's task for processing. If omitted, it has the value $ which designates the entire input. For more information, see Input and Output Processing).

** OutputPath (Optional)**
A path that selects a portion of the state's input to be passed to the state's output. If omitted, it has the value $ which designates the entire input. For more information, see Input and Output Processing.

Pass

A `Pass` state (`"Type"`: `"Pass"`) simply passes its input to its output, performing no work. `Pass` states are useful when constructing and debugging state machines.

In addition to the common state fields, `Pass` states allow the following fields:

** Result (Optional)**
Treated as the output of a virtual task to be passed on to the next state, and filtered as prescribed by the `ResultPath` field (if present).

** ResultPath (Optional)**
Specifies where (in the input) to place the "output" of the virtual task specified in `Result`. The input is further filtered as prescribed by the `OutputPath` field (if present) before being used as the state's output. For more information, see Input and Output Processing.

Here is an example of a `Pass` state that injects some fixed data into the state machine, probably for testing purposes.

```
1  "No-op": {
2    "Type": "Pass",
3    "Result": {
4      "x-datum": 0.381018,
5      "y-datum": 622.2269926397355
6    },
7    "ResultPath": "$.coords",
8    "Next": "End"
9  }
```

Suppose the input to this state is:

```
1  {
2    "georefOf": "Home"
3  }
```

Then the output would be:

```
1  {
2    "georefOf": "Home",
3    "coords": {
4      "x-datum": 0.381018,
5      "y-datum": 622.2269926397355
6    }
7  }
```

Task

A Task state (`"Type": "Task"`) represents a single unit of work performed by a state machine.

In addition to the common state fields, `Task` states have the following fields:

`Resource` (Required)
A URI, especially an Amazon Resource Name (ARN) that uniquely identifies the specific task to execute.

`ResultPath` (Optional)
Specifies where (in the input) to place the results of executing the task specified in `Resource`. The input is then filtered as prescribed by the `OutputPath` field (if present) before being used as the state's output. For more information, see path.

`Retry` (Optional)
An array of objects, called Retriers, that define a retry policy in case the state encounters runtime errors. For more information, see Retrying After an Error.

`Catch` (Optional)
An array of objects, called Catchers, that define a fallback state which is executed in case the state encounters runtime errors and its retry policy has been exhausted or is not defined. For more information, see Fallback States.

`TimeoutSeconds` (Optional)
If the task runs longer than the specified seconds, then this state fails with a `States.Timeout` Error Name. Must be a positive, non-zero integer. If not provided, the default value is `99999999`.

`HeartbeatSeconds` (Optional)
If more time than the specified seconds elapses between heartbeats from the task, then this state fails with an `States.Timeout` Error Name. Must be a positive, non-zero integer less than the number of seconds specified in the `TimeoutSeconds` field. If not provided, the default value is `99999999`.

A `Task` state must set either the `End` field to `true` if the state ends the execution, or must provide a state in the `Next` field that will be run upon completion of the `Task` state.

Here is an example:

```
1  "ActivityState": {
2    "Type": "Task",
3    "Resource": "arn:aws:states:us-east-1:123456789012:activity:HelloWorld",
4    "TimeoutSeconds": 300,
5    "HeartbeatSeconds": 60,
6    "Next": "NextState"
7  }
```

In this example, `ActivityState` will schedule the `HelloWorld` activity for execution in the `us-east-1` region on the caller's AWS account. When `HelloWorld` completes, the next state (here called `NextState`) will be run.

If this task fails to complete within 300 seconds, or does not send heartbeat notifications in intervals of 60 seconds, then the task is marked as `failed`. It's a good practice to set a timeout value and a heartbeat interval for long-running activities.

Specifying Resource ARNs in Tasks

The `Resource` field's Amazon Resource Name (ARN) is specified using the following pattern:

```
1  arn:partition:service:region:account:task_type:name
```

Where:

- `partition` is the AWS Step Functions partition to use, most commonly `aws`.
- `service` indicates the AWS service used to execute the task, and is either:
- `states` for an activity.
- `lambda` for a Lambda function.
- `region` is the AWS region in which the Step Functions activity/state machine type or Lambda function has been created.
- `account` is your AWS account id.
- `task_type` is the type of task to run. It will be one of the following values:
- `activity` – an activity.
- `function` – a Lambda function.
- `name` is the registered resource name (activity name or Lambda function name).

Note

Step Functions does not support referencing ARNs across partitions (For example: "aws-cn" cannot invoke tasks in the "aws" partition, and vice versa);

Task Types

The following task types are supported:

- activity
- Lambda functions

The following sections will provide more detail about each type.

Activity

Activities represent workers (processes or threads), implemented and hosted by you, that perform a specific task.

Activity `resource` ARNs use the following syntax:

```
1 arn:partition:states:region:account:activity:name
```

For more information about these fields, see Specifying Resource ARNs in Tasks.

Note

activities must be created with Step Functions (using a CreateActivity, API action, or the Step Functions console) before their first use.

For more information about creating an activity and implementing workers, see Activities.

Lambda Functions

Lambda functions execute a function using AWS Lambda. To specify a Lambda function, use the ARN of the Lambda function in the `Resource` field.

Lambda function `Resource` ARNs use the following syntax:

```
1 arn:partition:lambda:region:account:function:function_name
```

For more information about these fields, see Specifying Resource ARNs in Tasks.

For example:

```
1 "LambdaState": {
2   "Type": "Task",
3   "Resource": "arn:aws:lambda:us-east-1:123456789012:function:HelloWorld",
4   "Next": "NextState"
5 }
```

Once the Lambda function specified in the `Resource` field completes, its output is sent to the state identified in the `Next` field ("NextState").

Choice

A `Choice` state (`"Type": "Choice"`) adds branching logic to a state machine.

In addition to the common state fields, `Choice` states introduce the following additional fields:

** `Choices` (Required)**
An array of Choice Rules that determines which state the state machine transitions to next.

** `Default` (Optional, Recommended)**
The name of the state to transition to if none of the transitions in `Choices` is taken.

Important
`Choice` states do not support the `End` field. In addition, they use `Next` only inside their `Choices` field.

The following is an example of a `Choice` state and other states that it transitions to.

Note
You must specify the `$.type` field. If the state input doesn't contain the `$.type` field, the execution fails and an error is displayed in the execution history.

```
"ChoiceStateX": {
  "Type": "Choice",
  "Choices": [
    {
        "Not": {
          "Variable": "$.type",
          "StringEquals": "Private"
        },
        "Next": "Public"
    },
    {
      "Variable": "$.value",
      "NumericEquals": 0,
      "Next": "ValueIsZero"
    },
    {
      "And": [
        {
          "Variable": "$.value",
          "NumericGreaterThanEquals": 20
        },
        {
          "Variable": "$.value",
          "NumericLessThan": 30
        }
      ],
      "Next": "ValueInTwenties"
    }
  ],
  "Default": "DefaultState"
},

"Public": {
  "Type" : "Task",
  "Resource": "arn:aws:lambda:us-east-1:123456789012:function:Foo",
  "Next": "NextState"
```

```
37 },
38
39 "ValueIsZero": {
40   "Type" : "Task",
41   "Resource": "arn:aws:lambda:us-east-1:123456789012:function:Zero",
42   "Next": "NextState"
43 },
44
45 "ValueInTwenties": {
46   "Type" : "Task",
47   "Resource": "arn:aws:lambda:us-east-1:123456789012:function:Bar",
48   "Next": "NextState"
49 },
50
51 "DefaultState": {
52   "Type": "Fail",
53   "Cause": "No Matches!"
54 }
```

In this example the state machine starts with the following input value:

```
1 {
2   "type": "Private",
3   "value": 22
4 }
```

Step Functions transitions to the `ValueInTwenties` state, based on the `value` field.

If there are no matches for the `Choice` state's `Choices`, the state provided in the `Default` field runs instead. If the `Default` state isn't specified, the execution fails with an error.

Choice Rules

A `Choice` state must have a `Choices` field whose value is a non-empty array, whose every element is a object called a Choice Rule. A Choice Rule contains the following:

- **A comparison** – Two fields that specify an input variable to compared, the type of comparison, and the value to compare the variable to.
- **A Next field** – The value of this field must match a state name in the state machine.

The following example checks whether the numerical value is equal to 1:

```
1 {
2   "Variable": "$.foo",
3   "NumericEquals": 1,
4   "Next": "FirstMatchState"
5 }
```

The following example checks whether the string is equal to `MyString`:

```
1 {
2   "Variable": "$.foo",
3   "StringEquals": "MyString",
4   "Next": "FirstMatchState"
5 }
```

The following example checks whether the string is greater than `MyStringABC`:

```
1 {
2    "Variable": "$.foo",
3    "StringGreaterThan": "MyStringABC",
4    "Next": "FirstMatchState"
5 }
```

The following example checks whether the timestamp is equal to 2001-01-01T12:00:00Z:

```
1 {
2    "Variable": "$.foo",
3    "TimestampEquals": "2001-01-01T12:00:00Z",
4    "Next": "FirstMatchState"
5 }
```

Step Functions examines each of the Choice Rules in the order listed in the `Choices` field and transitions to the state specified in the `Next` field of the first Choice Rule in which the variable matches the value according to the comparison operator.

The following comparison operators are supported:

- `And`
- `BooleanEquals`
- `Not`
- `NumericEquals`
- `NumericGreaterThan`
- `NumericGreaterThanEquals`
- `NumericLessThan`
- `NumericLessThanEquals`
- `Or`
- `StringEquals`
- `StringGreaterThan`
- `StringGreaterThanEquals`
- `StringLessThan`
- `StringLessThanEquals`
- `TimestampEquals`
- `TimestampGreaterThan`
- `TimestampGreaterThanEquals`
- `TimestampLessThan`
- `TimestampLessThanEquals`

For each of these operators, the corresponding value must be of the appropriate type: string, number, Boolean, or timestamp. Step Functions doesn't attempt to match a numeric field to a string value. However, because timestamp fields are logically strings, it is possible that a field considered to be a timestamp can be matched by a `StringEquals` comparator.

Note
For interoperability, don't assume that numeric comparisons work with values outside the magnitude or precision that the IEEE 754-2008 `binary64` data type represents. In particular, integers outside of the range [-253+1, 253-1] might fail to compare in the expected way.
Timestamps (for example, 2016-08-18T17:33:00Z) must conform to RFC3339 profile ISO 8601, with further restrictions:
An uppercase `T` must separate the date and time portions. An uppercase `Z` must denote that a numeric time zone offset isn't present. To understand the behavior of string comparisons, see the Java `compareTo` documentation. The values of the `And` and `Or` operators must be non-empty arrays of Choice Rules that must not themselves contain `Next` fields. Likewise, the value of a `Not` operator must be a single Choice Rule that must not contain `Next` fields.

You can create complex, nested Choice Rules using **And**, **Not**, and **Or**. However, the **Next** field can appear only in a top-level Choice Rule.

Wait

A `Wait` state (`"Type": "Wait"`) delays the state machine from continuing for a specified time. You can choose either a relative time, specified in seconds from when the state begins, or an absolute end-time, specified as a timestamp.

In addition to the common state fields, `Wait` states have one of the following fields:

`Seconds`
A time, in seconds, to wait before beginning the state specified in the `Next` field.

`Timestamp`
An absolute time to wait until before beginning the state specified in the `Next` field.
Timestamps must conform to the RFC3339 profile of ISO 8601, with the further restrictions that an uppercase `T` must separate the date and time portions, and an uppercase `Z` must denote that a numeric time zone offset is not present, for example, `2016-08-18T17:33:00Z`.

`SecondsPath`
A time, in seconds, to wait before beginning the state specified in the `Next` field, specified using a path from the state's input data.

`TimestampPath`
An absolute time to wait until before beginning the state specified in the `Next` field, specified using a path from the state's input data.

Note
You must specify exactly one of `Seconds`, `Timestamp`, `SecondsPath`, or `TimestampPath`.

For example, the following `Wait` state introduces a ten second delay into a state machine:

```
1  "wait_ten_seconds": {
2    "Type": "Wait",
3    "Seconds": 10,
4    "Next": "NextState"
5  }
```

In the next example, the `Wait` state waits until an absolute time: March 14th, 2016, at 1:59 PM UTC.

```
1  "wait_until" : {
2    "Type": "Wait",
3    "Timestamp": "2016-03-14T01:59:00Z",
4    "Next": "NextState"
5  }
```

The wait duration does not have to be hard-coded. For example, given the following input data:

```
1  {
2    "expirydate": "2016-03-14T01:59:00Z"
3  }
```

You can select the value of "expirydate" from the input using a reference path to select it from the input data:

```
1  "wait_until" : {
2    "Type": "Wait",
3    "TimestampPath": "$.expirydate",
4    "Next": "NextState"
5  }
```

Succeed

A Succeed state ("Type": "Succeed") stops an execution successfully. The Succeed state is a useful target for Choice state branches that don't do anything but stop the execution.

Because Succeed states are terminal states, they have no Next field, nor do they have need of an End field, for example:

```
1 "SuccessState": {
2   "Type": "Succeed"
3 }
```

Fail

A Fail state ("Type": "Fail") stops the execution of the state machine and marks it as a failure.

The Fail state only allows the use of Type and Comment fields from the set of common state fields. In addition, the Fail state allows the following fields:

** Cause (Optional)**
Provides a custom failure string that can be used for operational or diagnostic purposes.

** Error (Optional)**
Provides an error name that can be used for error handling (Retry/Catch), operational or diagnostic purposes.

Because Fail states always exit the state machine, they have no Next field nor do they require an End field.

For example:

```
1 "FailState": {
2   "Type": "Fail",
3   "Cause": "Invalid response.",
4   "Error": "ErrorA"
5 }
```

Parallel

The `Parallel` state (`"Type"`: `"Parallel"`) can be used to create parallel branches of execution in your state machine.

In addition to the common state fields, `Parallel` states introduce these additional fields:

`Branches` (Required)
An array of objects that specify state machines to execute in parallel. Each such state machine object must have fields named `States` and `StartAt` whose meanings are exactly like those in the top level of a state machine.

`ResultPath` (Optional)
Specifies where (in the input) to place the output of the branches. The input is then filtered as prescribed by the `OutputPath` field (if present) before being used as the state's output. For more information, see Input and Output Processing.

`Retry` (Optional)
An array of objects, called Retriers that define a retry policy in case the state encounters runtime errors. For more information, see Retrying After an Error.

`Catch` (Optional)
An array of objects, called Catchers that define a fallback state which is executed in case the state encounters runtime errors and its retry policy has been exhausted or is not defined. For more information, see Fallback States.

A `Parallel` state causes AWS Step Functions to execute each branch, starting with the state named in that branch's `StartAt` field, as concurrently as possible, and wait until all branches terminate (reach a terminal state) before processing the `Parallel` state's `Next` field.

Here is an example:

```
 1  {
 2    "Comment": "Parallel Example.",
 3    "StartAt": "LookupCustomerInfo",
 4    "States": {
 5      "LookupCustomerInfo": {
 6        "Type": "Parallel",
 7        "End": true,
 8        "Branches": [
 9          {
10            "StartAt": "LookupAddress",
11            "States": {
12              "LookupAddress": {
13                "Type": "Task",
14                "Resource":
15                  "arn:aws:lambda:us-east-1:123456789012:function:AddressFinder",
16                "End": true
17              }
18            }
19          },
20          {
21            "StartAt": "LookupPhone",
22            "States": {
23              "LookupPhone": {
24                "Type": "Task",
25                "Resource":
26                  "arn:aws:lambda:us-east-1:123456789012:function:PhoneFinder",
27                "End": true
```

```
28              }
29            }
30          }
31        ]
32      }
33    }
34 }
```

In this example, the `LookupAddress` and `LookupPhone` branches are executed in parallel. Here is how the visual workflow looks in the Step Functions console:

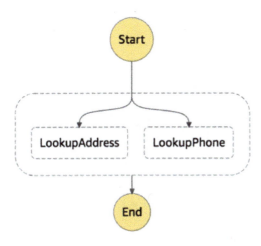

Each branch must be self-contained. A state in one branch of a `Parallel` state must not have a `Next` field that targets a field outside of that branch, nor can any other state outside the branch transition into that branch.

Parallel State Output

A `Parallel` state provides each branch with a copy of its own input data (subject to modification by the `InputPath` field). It generates output which is an array with one element for each branch containing the output from that branch. There is no requirement that all elements be of the same type. The output array can be inserted into the input data (and the whole sent as the `Parallel` state's output) by using a `ResultPath` field in the usual way (see Input and Output Processing).

Here is another example:

```
1 {
2   "Comment": "Parallel Example.",
3   "StartAt": "FunWithMath",
4   "States": {
5     "FunWithMath": {
6     "Type": "Parallel",
7     "End": true,
```

```
 8      "Branches": [
 9        {
10          "StartAt": "Add",
11          "States": {
12            "Add": {
13              "Type": "Task",
14              "Resource": "arn:aws:swf:us-east-1:123456789012:task:Add",
15              "End": true
16            }
17          }
18        },
19        {
20          "StartAt": "Subtract",
21          "States": {
22            "Subtract": {
23              "Type": "Task",
24              "Resource": "arn:aws:swf:us-east-1:123456789012:task:Subtract",
25              "End": true
26            }
27          }
28        }
29      ]
30    }
31  }
32 }
```

If the FunWithMath state was given the array [3, 2] as input, then both the Add and Subtract states receive that array as input. The output of Add would be 5, that of Subtract would be 1, and the output of the Parallel state would be an array:

```
1 [ 5, 1 ]
```

Error Handling

If any branch fails, due to either an unhandled error or by transitioning to a Fail state, the entire Parallel state is considered to have failed and all its branches are stopped. If the error is not handled by the Parallel state itself, Step Functions will stop the execution with an error.

Input and Output Processing

In this section you will learn how to use paths and reference paths for input and output processing.

Note
For an overview, see Input and Output Processing in Step Functions in the How Step Functions Works section.

Paths

In Amazon States Language, a *path* is a string beginning with $ that you can use to identify components within JSON text. Paths follow JsonPath syntax.

Reference Paths

A *reference path* is a path whose syntax is limited in such a way that it can identify only a single node in a JSON structure:

- You can access object fields using only dot (.) and square bracket ([ ]) notation.
- The operators @ .. , : ? * aren't supported.
- Functions such as length() aren't supported.

For example, state input data contains the following values:

```
1 {
2     "foo": 123,
3     "bar": ["a", "b", "c"],
4     "car": {
5         "cdr": true
6     }
7 }
```

In this case, the following reference paths would return:

```
1 $.foo => 123
2 $.bar => ["a", "b", "c"]
3 $.car.cdr => true
```

Certain states use paths and reference paths to control the flow of a state machine or configure a states's settings or options.

Paths in InputPath, ResultPath, and OutputPath Fields

To specify how to use part of the state's input and what to send as output to the next state, you can use InputPath, OutputPath, and ResultPath:

- For InputPath and OutputPath, you must use a path that follows the JsonPath syntax.
- For ResultPath, you must use a reference path.

InputPath

The InputPath field selects a portion of the state's input to pass to the state's task for processing. If you omit the field, it gets the $ value, representing the entire input. If you use null, the input is discarded (not sent to the state's task) and the task receives JSON text representing an empty object {}.

Note

A path can yield a selection of values. Consider the following example:

```
1 { "a": [1, 2, 3, 4] }
```

If you apply the path `$.a[0:2]`, the following is the result:

```
1 [ 1, 2 ]
```

ResultPath

Usually, if a state executes a task, the task results are sent along as the state's output (which becomes the input for the next task).

If a state doesn't execute a task, the state's own input is sent, unmodified, as its output. However, when you specify a path in the value of a state's `ResultPath` and `OutputPath` fields, different scenarios become possible.

The `ResultPath` takes the results of executing the state's task and places them in the input. Next, the `OutputPath` selects a portion of the input to send as the state's output. The `ResultPath` might add the results of executing the state's task to the input, overwrite an existing part, or overwrite the entire input:

- If the `ResultPath` matches an item in the state's input, only that input item is overwritten with the results of executing the state's task. The entire modified input becomes available to the state's output.
- If the `ResultPath` doesn't match an item in the state's input, an item is added to the input. The item contains the results of executing the state's task. The expanded input becomes available to the state's output.
- If the `ResultPath` has the default value of `$`, it matches the entire input. In this case, the results of the state execution overwrite the input entirely and the input becomes available to pass along.
- If the `ResultPath` is `null`, the results of executing the state are discarded and the input is untouched.

Note

`ResultPath` field values must be reference paths. For more information on `ResultPath` see Understanding `ResultPath`

OutputPath

- If the `OutputPath` matches an item in the state's input, only that input item is selected. This input item becomes the state's output.
- If the `OutputPath` doesn't match an item in the state's input, an exception specifies an invalid path. For more information, see Errors.
- If the `OutputPath` has the default value of `$`, this matches the entire input completely. In this case, the entire input is passed to the next state.
- If the `OutputPath` is `null`, JSON text representing an empty object `{}` is sent to the next state.

The following example demonstrates how `InputPath`, `ResultPath`, and `OutputPath` fields work in practice. Consider the following input for the current state:

```
1 {
2   "title": "Numbers to add",
3   "numbers": { "val1": 3, "val2": 4 }
4 }
```

In addition, the state has the following `InputPath`, `ResultPath`, and `OutputPath` fields:

```
1 "InputPath": "$.numbers",
2 "ResultPath": "$.sum",
3 "OutputPath": "$"
```

The state's task receives only the `numbers` object from the input. In turn, if this task returns 7, the output of this state is as follows:

```
1 {
2   "title": "Numbers to add",
3   "numbers": { "val1": 3, "val2": 4 }
4   "sum": 7
5 }
```

You can slightly modify the `OutputPath`:

```
1 "InputPath": "$.numbers",
2 "ResultPath": "$.sum",
3 "OutputPath": "$.sum"
```

As before, you use the following state input data:

```
1 {
2   "numbers": { "val1": 3, "val2": 4 }
3 }
```

However, now the state output data is 7.

Errors

Any state can encounter runtime errors. Errors can arise because of state machine definition issues (for example, no matching rule in a `Choice` state), task failures (for example, an exception from a Lambda function) or because of transient issues, such as network partition events. When a state reports an error, the default course of action for AWS Step Functions is to fail the execution entirely.

Error Representation

Errors are identified in Amazon States Language by case-sensitive strings, called Error Names. Amazon States Language defines a set of built-in strings naming well-known errors, all of which begin with the prefix "States.":

Predefined Error Codes

** `States.ALL` **
A wild-card that matches any Error Name.

** `States.Timeout` **
A `Task` state either ran longer than the "TimeoutSeconds" value, or failed to send a heartbeat for a time longer than the "HeartbeatSeconds" value.

** `States.TaskFailed` **
A `Task` state failed during the execution.

** `States.Permissions` **
A `Task` state failed because it had insufficient privileges to execute the specified code.

States may report errors with other names, which must not begin with the prefix "States.".

Retrying After an Error

`Task` and `Parallel` states may have a field named `Retry`, whose value must be an array of objects, called Retriers. An individual Retrier represents a certain number of retries, usually at increasing time intervals.

Note
Retries are treated as state transitions. For information on how state transitions affect billing, see Step Functions Pricing.

A Retrier contains the following fields:

** `ErrorEquals` (Required)**
A non-empty array of Strings that match Error Names. When a state reports an error, Step Functions scans through the Retriers and, when the Error Name appears in this array, it implements the retry policy described in this Retrier.

** `IntervalSeconds` (Optional)**
An integer that represents the number of seconds before the first retry attempt (default 1).

** `MaxAttempts` (Optional)**
A positive integer, representing the maximum number of retry attempts (default 3). If the error recurs more times than specified, retries cease and normal error handling resumes. A value of 0 is permitted and indicates that the error or errors should never be retried.

** `BackoffRate` (Optional)**
A number that is the multiplier by which the retry interval increases on each attempt (default 2.0).

Here is an example of a Retry field that will make 2 retry attempts after waits of 3 and 4.5 seconds:

```
1  "Retry" : [
2     {
3        "ErrorEquals": [ "States.Timeout" ],
4        "IntervalSeconds": 3,
5        "MaxAttempts": 2,
6        "BackoffRate": 1.5
7     }
8  ]
```

The reserved name `States.ALL` appearing in a Retrier's `ErrorEquals` field is a wildcard that matches any Error Name. It must appear alone in the `ErrorEquals` array and must appear in the last Retrier in the `Retry` array.

Here is an example of a `Retry` field that will retry any error except for `States.Timeout`:

```
1  "Retry" : [
2    {
3      "ErrorEquals": [ "States.Timeout" ],
4      "MaxAttempts": 0
5    },
6    {
7      "ErrorEquals": [ "States.ALL" ]
8    }
9  ]
```

Complex Retry Scenarios

A Retrier's parameters apply across all visits to that Retrier in the context of a single state execution. This is best illustrated by an example; consider the following Task state:

```
1  "X": {
2    "Type": "Task",
3    "Resource": "arn:aws:states:us-east-1:123456789012:task:X",
4    "Next": "Y",
5    "Retry": [
6      {
7        "ErrorEquals": [ "ErrorA", "ErrorB" ],
8        "IntervalSeconds": 1,
9        "BackoffRate": 2.0,
10       "MaxAttempts": 2
11     },
12     {
13       "ErrorEquals": [ "ErrorC" ],
14       "IntervalSeconds": 5
15     }
16   ],
17   "Catch": [
18     {
19       "ErrorEquals": [ "States.ALL" ],
20       "Next": "Z"
21     }
22   ]
23 }
```

Suppose that this task fails five successive times, outputting Error Names "ErrorA", "ErrorB", "ErrorC", "ErrorB", and "ErrorB". The first two errors match the first retrier, and cause waits of one and two seconds.

The third error matches the second retrier, and causes a wait of five seconds. The fourth error matches the first retrier and causes a wait of four seconds. The fifth error also matches the first retrier, but it has already reached its limit of two retries ("MaxAttempts") for that particular error ("ErrorB") so it fails and execution is redirected to the "Z" state via the "Catch" field.

Note that once the system transitions to another state, no matter how, all Retrier parameters are reset.

Note
You can generate custom error names (such as ErrorA and ErrorB above) using either an activity or Lambda functions. For more information, see Handling Error Conditions Using a State Machine.

Fallback States

Task and Parallel states may have a field named Catch, whose value must be an array of objects, called Catchers.

A Catcher contains the following fields:

** ErrorEquals (Required)**
A non-empty array of Strings that match Error Names, specified exactly as with the Retrier field of the same name.

** Next (Required)**
A string which must exactly match one of the state machine's state names.

** ResultPath (Optional)**
A path which determines what is sent as input to the state specified by the Next field.

When a state reports an error and either there is no Retry field, or retries have failed to resolve the error, AWS Step Functions scans through the Catchers in the order listed in the array, and when the Error Name appears in the value of a Catcher's ErrorEquals field, the state machine transitions to the state named in the Next field.

The reserved name States.ALL appearing in a Catcher's ErrorEquals field is a wildcard that matches any Error Name. It must appear alone in the ErrorEquals array and must appear in the last Catcher in the Catch array.

Here is an example of a Catch field that will transition to the state named "RecoveryState" when a Lambda function outputs an unhandled Java exception, and otherwise to the "EndState" state.

```
 1 "Catch": [
 2   {
 3     "ErrorEquals": [ "java.lang.Exception" ],
 4     "ResultPath": "$.error-info",
 5     "Next": "RecoveryState"
 6   },
 7   {
 8     "ErrorEquals": [ "States.ALL" ],
 9     "Next": "EndState"
10   }
11 ]
```

Each Catcher can specify multiple errors to handle.

When AWS Step Functions transitions to the state specified in a Catcher, it sends along as input JSON text that is different than what it would normally send to the next state when there was no error. This JSON text represents an object containing a field "Error" whose value is a string containing the error name. The object will also, usually, contain a field "Cause" that has a human-readable description of the error. We refer to this object as the Error Output.

In this example, the first Catcher contains a ResultPath field. This works in a similar fashion to a ResultPath field in a state's top level—it takes the results of executing the state and overwrites a portion of the state's input, or all of the state's input, or it takes the results and adds them to the input. In the case of an error handled by a Catcher, the result of executing the state is the Error Output.

So in the example, for the first Catcher the Error Output will be added to the input as a field named `error -info` (assuming there is not already a field by that name in the input) and the entire input will be sent to `RecoveryState`. For the second Catcher, the Error Output will overwrite the input and so just the Error Output will be sent to `EndState`. When not specified, the `ResultPath` field defaults to `$` which selects, and so overwrites, the entire input.

When a state has both Retry and Catch fields, Step Functions uses any appropriate Retriers first and only applies the matching Catcher transition if the retry policy fails to resolve the error.

Best Practices for Step Functions

The following best practices for implementing Step Functions workflows can help you optimize the performance of your implementations.

Topics

- Use Timeouts to Avoid Stuck Executions
- Use ARNs Instead of Passing Large Payloads
- Avoid Reaching the History Limit

Use Timeouts to Avoid Stuck Executions

By default, the Amazon States Language doesn't set timeouts in state machine definitions. Without an explicit timeout, Step Functions often relies solely on a response from an activity worker to know that a task is complete. If something goes wrong and `TimeoutSeconds` isn't specified, an execution is stuck waiting for a response that will never come.

To avoid this, specify a reasonable timeout limit when you create a task in your state machine. For example:

```
1  "ActivityState": {
2    "Type": "Task",
3    "Resource": "arn:aws:states:us-east-1:123456789012:activity:HelloWorld",
4    "TimeoutSeconds": 300,
5    "HeartbeatSeconds": 60,
6    "Next": "NextState"
7  }
```

For more information, see Task in the Amazon States Language documentation.

Use ARNs Instead of Passing Large Payloads

Executions that pass large payloads of data between states can be terminated. If the data you are passing between states might grow to over 32 K, use Amazon Simple Storage Service (Amazon S3) to store the data, and pass the Amazon Resource Name instead of the raw data. Alternatively, adjust your implementation so that you pass smaller payloads in your executions.

For more information, see:

- Amazon Simple Storage Service Developer Guide
- Amazon Resource Names (ARNs)

Avoid Reaching the History Limit

AWS Step Functions has a hard limit of 25,000 entries in the execution history. To avoid reaching this limit for long-running executions, implement a pattern that uses an AWS Lambda function that can start a new execution of your state machine to split ongoing work across multiple workflow executions.

For more information, see the Continue as a New Execution tutorial.

Limits

AWS Step Functions places limits on the sizes of certain state machine parameters, such as the number of API actions that you can make during a certain time period or the number of state machines that you can define. Although these limits are designed to prevent a misconfigured state machine from consuming all of the resources of the system, they aren't hard limits.

Note
If a particular stage of your state machine execution or activity execution takes too long, you can configure a state machine timeout to cause a timeout event.

Topics

- General Limits
- Limits Related to Accounts
- Limits Related to State Machine Executions
- Limits Related to Task Executions
- Limits Related to API Action Throttling
- Limits Related to State Throttling
- Requesting a Limit Increase

General Limits

Limit	Description
State machine name	State machine names must be 1–80 characters in length, must be unique for your account and region, and must not contain any of the following: [See the AWS documentation website for more details] Step Functions allows you to create state machine, execution, and activity names that contain non-ASCII characters. These non-ASCII names don't work with Amazon CloudWatch. To ensure that you can track CloudWatch metrics, choose a name that uses only ASCII characters.

Limits Related to Accounts

Limit	Description
Maximum number of registered activities	10,000
Maximum number of registered state machines	10,000
Maximum number of API actions	Beyond infrequent spikes, applications may be throttled if they make a large number of API actions in a very short period of time.
Maximum request size	1 MB per request. This is the total data size per Step Functions API request, including the request header and all other associated request data.

Limits Related to State Machine Executions

Limit	Description
Maximum open executions	1,000,000
Maximum execution time	1 year. If an execution runs for more than the 1 year limit, it will fail with a `States.Timeout` error and emit a `ExecutionsTimedout` CloudWatch metric.
Maximum execution history size	25,000 events
Maximum execution idle time	1 year (constrained by execution time limit)
Maximum execution history retention time	90 days. After this time, you can no longer retrieve or view the execution history. There is no further limit to the number of closed executions that Step Functions retains.
Maximum executions displayed in Step Functions console	The Step Functions console displays a maximum of 1,000 executions per state machine. If you have more than 1,000 executions, use the Step Functions API actions or the AWS CLI to display all of your executions.

Limits Related to Task Executions

Limit	Description
Maximum task execution time	1 year (constrained by execution time limit)
Maximum time Step Functions keeps a task in the queue	1 year (constrained by execution time limit)
Maximum open activities	1,000 per execution. This limit includes both activities that have been scheduled and those being processed by workers.
Maximum input or result data size for a task, state, or execution	32,768 characters. This limit affects tasks (activity or Lambda function), state or execution result data, and input data when scheduling a task, entering a state, or starting an execution.

Limits Related to API Action Throttling

Some Step Functions API actions are throttled using a token bucket scheme to maintain service bandwidth.

Note
Throttling limits are per account, per region. AWS Step Functions may increase both the bucket size and refill rate at any time. Do not rely on these throttling rates to limit your costs.

API Name	Bucket Size	Refill Rate per Second
CreateActivity	100	1
CreateStateMachine	100	1
DeleteActivity	100	1
DeleteStateMachine	100	1

API Name	Bucket Size	Refill Rate per Second
DescribeActivity	200	1
DescribeExecution	200	2
DescribeStateMachine	200	1
DescribeStateMachineForExecution	100	1
GetActivityTask	1,000	25
GetExecutionHistory	250	5
ListActivities	100	1
ListExecutions	100	2
ListStateMachines	100	1
SendTaskFailure	1,000	25
SendTaskHeartbeat	1,000	25
SendTaskSuccess	1,000	25
StartExecution — In US East (N. Virginia), US West (Oregon), and EU (Ireland)	1000	200
StartExecution — All other regions	500	25
StopExecution — In US East (N. Virginia), US West (Oregon), and EU (Ireland)	1000	200
StopExecution — All other regions	500	25
UpdateStateMachine	200	1

Limits Related to State Throttling

Step Functions state transitions are throttled using a token bucket scheme to maintain service bandwidth.

Note
Throttling on the `StateTransition` service metric is reported as `ExecutionThrottled` in CloudWatch. For more information, see the `ExecutionThrottled` CloudWatch metric.

Service Metric	Bucket Size	Refill Rate per Second
`StateTransition` — *In US East (N. Virginia), US West (Oregon), and EU (Ireland)*	5000	1000
`StateTransition` — *All other regions*	800	400

Requesting a Limit Increase

Use the **Support Center** page in the AWS Management Console to request a limit increase for resources provided by AWS Step Functions on a per-region basis. For more information, see To Request a Limit Increase in the *AWS General Reference.*

Monitoring and Logging

This section provides information about monitoring and logging Step Functions.

Topics

- Monitoring Step Functions Using CloudWatch
- Logging Step Functions using CloudTrail

Monitoring Step Functions Using CloudWatch

Monitoring is an important part of maintaining the reliability, availability, and performance of AWS Step Functions and your AWS solutions. You should collect as much monitoring data from the AWS services that you use so that you can more easily debug any multi-point failures. Before you start monitoring Step Functions, you should create a monitoring plan that answers the following questions:

- What are your monitoring goals?
- What resources will you monitor?
- How often will you monitor these resources?
- What monitoring tools will you use?
- Who will perform the monitoring tasks?
- Who should be notified when something goes wrong?

The next step is to establish a baseline for normal Step Functions performance in your environment. To do this, measure performance at various times and under different load conditions. As you monitor Step Functions, you should consider storing historical monitoring data. Such data can give you a baseline to compare against current performance data, to identify normal performance patterns and performance anomalies, and to devise ways to address issues.

For example, with Step Functions, you can monitor how many activities or Lambda tasks fail due to a heartbeat timeout. When performance falls outside your established baseline, you might have to change your heartbeat interval.

To establish a baseline you should, at a minimum, monitor the following metrics:

- `ActivitiesStarted`
- `ActivitiesTimedOut`
- `ExecutionsStarted`
- `ExecutionsTimedOut`
- `LambdaFunctionsStarted`
- `LambdaFunctionsTimedOut`

The following sections describe metrics that Step Functions provides to CloudWatch. You can use these metrics to track your state machines and activities and to set alarms on threshold values. You can view metrics using the AWS Management Console.

Topics

- Metrics that Report a Time Interval
- Metrics that Report a Count
- State Machine Metrics
- Viewing Metrics for Step Functions
- Setting Alarms for Step Functions

Metrics that Report a Time Interval

Some of the Step Functions CloudWatch metrics are *time intervals*, always measured in milliseconds. These metrics generally correspond to stages of your execution for which you can set state machine, activity, and Lambda function timeouts, with descriptive names.

For example, the `ActivityRunTime` metric measures the time it takes for an activity to complete after it begins to execute. You can set a timeout value for the same time period.

In the CloudWatch console, you can get the best results if you choose **average** as the display statistic for time interval metrics.

Metrics that Report a Count

Some of the Step Functions CloudWatch metrics report results as a *count*. For example, `ExecutionsFailed` records the number of failed state machine executions.

In the CloudWatch console, you can get the best results if you choose **sum** as the display statistic for count metrics.

State Machine Metrics

The following metrics are available for Step Functions state machines:

Execution Metrics

The `AWS/States` namespace includes the following metrics for Step Functions executions:

Metric	Description
ExecutionTime	The interval, in milliseconds, between the time the execution starts and the time it closes.
ExecutionThrottled	The number of StateEntered events and retries that have been throttled. This is related to StateTransition throttling. For more information, see Limits Related to State Throttling in the AWS Step Functions Developer Guide.
ExecutionsAborted	The number of aborted or terminated executions.
ExecutionsFailed	The number of failed executions.
ExecutionsStarted	The number of started executions.
ExecutionsSucceeded	The number of successfully completed executions.
ExecutionsTimedOut	The number of executions that time out for any reason.

Dimension for Step Functions Execution Metrics

Dimension	Description
StateMachineArn	The ARN of the state machine for the execution in question.

Activity Metrics

The `AWS/States` namespace includes the following metrics for Step Functions activities:

Metric	Description
ActivityRunTime	The interval, in milliseconds, between the time the activity starts and the time it closes.
ActivityScheduleTime	The interval, in milliseconds, for which the activity stays in the schedule state.

Metric	Description
ActivityTime	The interval, in milliseconds, between the time the activity is scheduled and the time it closes.
ActivitiesFailed	The number of failed activities.
ActivitiesHeartbeatTimedOut	The number of activities that time out due to a heartbeat timeout.
ActivitiesScheduled	The number of scheduled activities.
ActivitiesStarted	The number of started activities.
ActivitiesSucceeded	The number of successfully completed activities.
ActivitiesTimedOut	The number of activities that time out on close.

Dimension for Step Functions Activity Metrics

Dimension	Description
ActivityArn	The ARN of the activity.

Lambda Function Metrics

The `AWS/States` namespace includes the following metrics for Step Functions Lambda functions:

Metric	Description
LambdaFunctionRunTime	The interval, in milliseconds, between the time the Lambda function starts and the time it closes.
LambdaFunctionScheduleTime	The interval, in milliseconds, for which the Lambda function stays in the schedule state.
LambdaFunctionTime	The interval, in milliseconds, between the time the Lambda function is scheduled and the time it closes.
LambdaFunctionsFailed	The number of failed Lambda functions.
LambdaFunctionsHeartbeatTimedOut	The number of Lambda functions that time out due to a heartbeat timeout.
LambdaFunctionsScheduled	The number of scheduled Lambda functions.
LambdaFunctionsStarted	The number of started Lambda functions.
LambdaFunctionsSucceeded	The number of successfully completed Lambda functions.
LambdaFunctionsTimedOut	The number of Lambda functions that time out on close.

Dimension for Step Functions Lambda Function Metrics

Dimension	Description
LambdaFunctionArn	The ARN of the Lambda function.

Service Metrics

The `AWS/States` namespace includes the following metrics for the Step Functions service:

Metric	Description
ThrottledEvents	The count of requests that have been throttled.
ProvisionedBucketSize	The count of available requests per second.
ProvisionedRefillRate	The count of requests per second that are allowed into the bucket.
ConsumedCapacity	The count of requests per second.

Dimension for Step Functions Service Metrics

Dimension	Description
StateTransition	Filters data to show State Transitions metrics.

API Metrics

The `AWS/States` namespace includes the following metrics for the Step Functions API:

Metric	Description
ThrottledEvents	The count of requests that have been throttled.
ProvisionedBucketSize	The count of available requests per second.
ProvisionedRefillRate	The count of requests per second that are allowed into the bucket.
ConsumedCapacity	The count of requests per second.

Dimension for Step Functions API Metrics

Dimension	Description
APIName	Filters data to an API of the specified API name.

Viewing Metrics for Step Functions

1. Open the AWS Management Console and navigate to **CloudWatch**.

2. Choose **Metrics** and on the **All Metrics** tab, choose **States**.

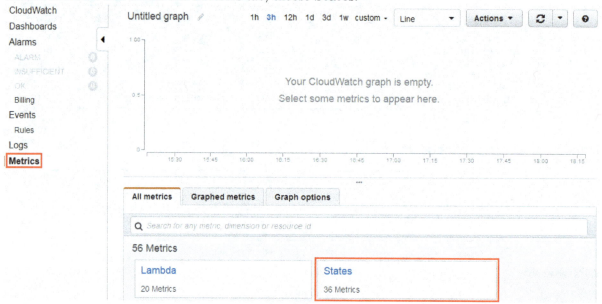

If you ran any executions recently, you will see up to three types of metrics:

- **Execution Metrics**
- **Activity Function Metrics**
- **Lambda Function Metrics**

3. Choose a metric type to see a list of metrics.

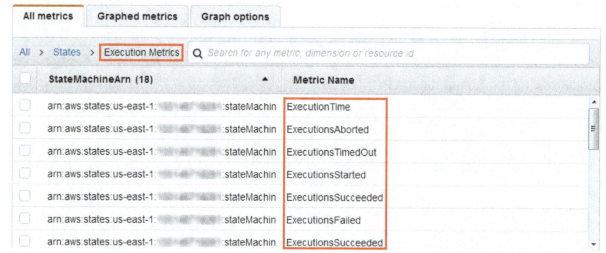

- To sort your metrics by **Metric Name** or **StateMachineArn**, use the column headings.

- To view graphs for a metric, choose the box next to the metric on the list. You can change the graph parameters using the time range controls above the graph view.

  You can choose custom time ranges using relative or absolute values (specific days and times). You can also use the drop-down list to display values as lines, stacked areas, or numbers (values).

- To view the details about a graph, hover over the metric color code which appears below the graph.

  ■ ExecutionsAborted   ■ ExecutionsStarted   ■ ExecutionsSucceeded   ■ ExecutionsTimedOut

The metric's details are displayed.

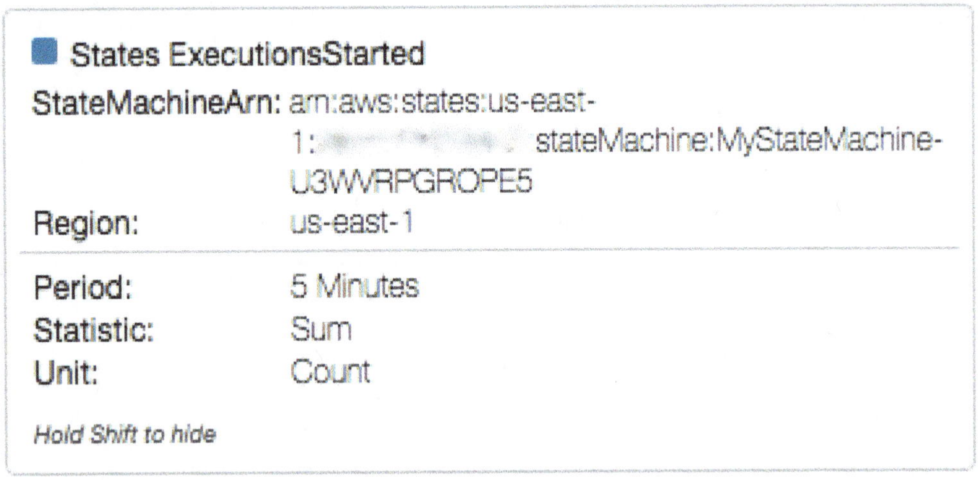

■ States ExecutionsStarted

StateMachineArn: arn:aws:states:us-east-
                 1:_____ stateMachine:MyStateMachine-
                 U3WVRPGROPE5
Region: us-east-1

Period: 5 Minutes
Statistic: Sum
Unit: Count

Hold Shift to hide

For more information about working with CloudWatch metrics, see Using Amazon CloudWatch Metrics in the *Amazon CloudWatch User Guide*.

Setting Alarms for Step Functions

You can use CloudWatch alarms to perform actions. For example, if you want to know when an alarm threshold is reached, you can set an alarm to send a notification to an Amazon SNS topic or to send an email when the `StateMachinesFailed` metric rises above a certain threshold.

To set an alarm on a metric

1. Open the AWS Management Console and navigate to **CloudWatch**.

2. Choose **Metrics** and on the **All Metrics** tab, choose **States**.

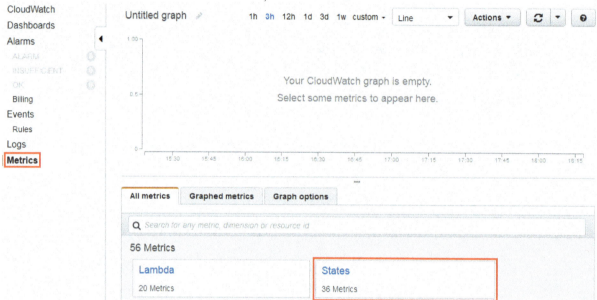

If you ran any executions recently, you will see up to three types of metrics:

- **Execution Metrics**
- **Activity Function Metrics**
- **Lambda Function Metrics**

3. Choose a metric type to see a list of metrics.

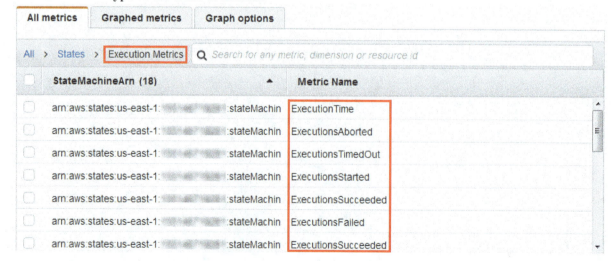

4. Choose a metric and then choose **Graphed metrics**.

5. Choose 🔔 next to a metric on the list.

Label	Namespace	Dimensions	Metric Na...	Statistic ▽	Period ▽	Y Axis	Actions ▽
● E...	AWS/States	Dimensions (1)	ExecutionTim‹	Average	5 Minutes	‹ ›	🔔 ⧉ ✖

The **Create Alarm** dialog box is displayed.

Create Alarm   ✕

1. Select Metric   **2. Define Alarm**

Alarm Threshold

Provide the details and threshold for your alarm. Use the graph on the right to help set the appropriate threshold.

Name: [   ]

Description: [   ]

Whenever: ExecutionTime

is: [>= ▼] [0   ]

for: [1] consecutive period(s)

Actions

Define what actions are taken when your alarm changes state.

Notification   Delete

Whenever this alarm: [State is ALARM   ▼]

Send notification to: [Select a notification list ▼] New list Enter list ⓘ

[+ Notification] [+ AutoScaling Action] [+ EC2 Action]

Alarm Preview

This alarm will trigger when the blue line goes up to or above the red line for a duration of 5 minutes

ExecutionTime >= 0

50
40
30
20
10
0
  11/18   11/18   11/18
  16:00   17:00   18:00

Namespace: AWS/States

StateMachine-Arn: [arn:aws:states:us-east-1]

Metric Name: [ExecutionTime]

Period: [5 Minutes ▼]

Statistic: ◉ Standard ○ Custom

[Average ▼]

Cancel   [Previous]   Next   [**Create Alarm**]

6. Enter the values for the **Alarm threshold** and **Actions** and then choose **Create Alarm**.

For more information about setting and using CloudWatch alarms, see Creating Amazon CloudWatch Alarms in the *Amazon CloudWatch User Guide*.

Logging Step Functions using CloudTrail

AWS Step Functions is integrated with CloudTrail, a service that captures specific API calls and delivers log files to an Amazon S3 bucket that you specify. With the information collected by CloudTrail, you can determine what request was made to Step Functions, the IP address from which the request was made, who made the request, when it was made, and so on.

To learn more about CloudTrail, including how to configure and enable it, see the AWS CloudTrail User Guide.

Step Functions Information in CloudTrail

When CloudTrail logging is enabled in your AWS account, API actions made to specific Step Functions actions are tracked in CloudTrail log files. Step Functions actions are written, together with other AWS service records. CloudTrail determines when to create and write to a new file based on a time period and file size.

The following actions are supported:

- CreateActivity
- CreateStateMachine
- DeleteActivity
- DeleteStateMachine
- StartExecution
- StopExecution

Every log entry contains information about who generated the request. The user identity information in the log helps you determine the following:

- Whether the request was made with root or IAM user credentials
- Whether the request was made with temporary security credentials for a role or federated user
- Whether the request was made by another AWS service

For more information, see the userIdentity element in the *AWS CloudTrail User Guide*.

You can store your log files in your S3 bucket for as long as you want, but you can also define Amazon S3 lifecycle rules to archive or delete log files automatically. By default, your log files are encrypted with Amazon S3 server-side encryption.

If you want to be notified upon log file delivery, you can configure CloudTrail to publish Amazon SNS notifications when new log files are delivered. For more information, see Configuring Amazon SNS Notifications for CloudTrail.

You can also aggregate Step Functions log files from multiple AWS regions and multiple AWS accounts into a single Amazon S3 bucket. For more information, see Receiving CloudTrail Log Files from Multiple Regions and Receiving CloudTrail Log Files from Multiple Accounts.

Understanding Step Functions Log File Entries

CloudTrail log files contain one or more log entries. Each entry lists multiple JSON-formatted events. A log entry represents a single request from any source and includes information about the requested action, the date and time of the action, request parameters, and so on. The log entries are not an ordered stack trace of the public API actions, so they do not appear in any specific order.

CreateActivity

The following example shows a CloudTrail log entry that demonstrates the CreateActivity action:

```
1  {
2      "eventVersion": "1.04",
3      "userIdentity": {
4          "type": "IAMUser",
5          "principalId": "AIDAJYDLDBVBI4EXAMPLE",
6          "arn": "arn:aws:iam::123456789012:user/test-user",
7          "accountId": "123456789012",
8          "accessKeyId": "AKIAIOSFODNN7EXAMPLE",
9          "userName": "test-user"
10     },
11     "eventTime": "2016-10-28T01:17:56Z",
12     "eventSource": "states.amazonaws.com",
13     "eventName": "CreateActivity",
14     "awsRegion": "us-east-1",
15     "sourceIPAddress": "10.61.88.189",
16     "userAgent": "Coral/Netty",
17     "requestParameters": {
18         "name": "OtherActivityPrefix.2016-10-27-18-16-56.894c791e-2ced-4cf4-8523-376469410c25"
19     },
20     "responseElements": {
21         "activityArn": "arn:aws:states:us-east-1:123456789012:activity:OtherActivityPrefix
                 .2016-10-27-18-16-56.894c791e-2ced-4cf4-8523-376469410c25",
22         "creationDate": "Oct 28, 2016 1:17:56 AM"
23     },
24     "requestID": "37c67602-9cac-11e6-aed5-5b57d226e9ef",
25     "eventID": "dc3becef-d06d-49bf-bc93-9b76b5f00774",
26     "eventType": "AwsApiCall",
27     "recipientAccountId": "123456789012"
28 }
```

CreateStateMachine

The following example shows a CloudTrail log entry that demonstrates the CreateStateMachine action:

```
1  {
2      "eventVersion": "1.04",
3      "userIdentity": {
4          "type": "IAMUser",
5          "principalId": "AIDAJYDLDBVBI4EXAMPLE",
6          "arn": "arn:aws:iam::123456789012:user/test-user",
7          "accountId": "123456789012",
8          "accessKeyId": "AKIAJL5C75K4ZEXAMPLE",
9          "userName": "test-user"
10     },
11     "eventTime": "2016-10-28T01:18:07Z",
12     "eventSource": "states.amazonaws.com",
13     "eventName": "CreateStateMachine",
14     "awsRegion": "us-east-1",
15     "sourceIPAddress": "10.61.88.189",
16     "userAgent": "Coral/Netty",
17     "requestParameters": {
18         "name": "testUser.2016-10-27-18-17-06.bd144e18-0437-476e-9bb",
19         "roleArn": "arn:aws:iam::123456789012:role/graphene/tests/graphene-execution-role",
```

```
20        "definition": "{   \"StartAt\": \"SinglePass\",   \"States\": {       \"SinglePass\": {
                   \"Type\": \"Pass\",            \"End\": true       }  }}"
21      },
22      "responseElements": {
23          "stateMachineArn": "arn:aws:states:us-east-1:123456789012:stateMachine:testUser
                  .2016-10-27-18-17-06.bd144e18-0437-476e-9bb",
24          "creationDate": "Oct 28, 2016 1:18:07 AM"
25      },
26      "requestID": "3da6370c-9cac-11e6-aed5-5b57d226e9ef",
27      "eventID": "84a0441d-fa06-4691-a60a-aab9e46d689c",
28      "eventType": "AwsApiCall",
29      "recipientAccountId": "123456789012"
30  }
```

DeleteActivity

The following example shows a CloudTrail log entry that demonstrates the DeleteActivity action:

```
1  {
2      "eventVersion": "1.04",
3      "userIdentity": {
4          "type": "IAMUser",
5          "principalId": "AIDAJYDLDBVBI4EXAMPLE",
6          "arn": "arn:aws:iam::123456789012:user/test-user",
7          "accountId": "123456789012",
8          "accessKeyId": "AKIAJL5C75K4ZEXAMPLE",
9          "userName": "test-user"
10     },
11     "eventTime": "2016-10-28T01:18:27Z",
12     "eventSource": "states.amazonaws.com",
13     "eventName": "DeleteActivity",
14     "awsRegion": "us-east-1",
15     "sourceIPAddress": "10.61.88.189",
16     "userAgent": "Coral/Netty",
17     "requestParameters": {
18         "activityArn": "arn:aws:states:us-east-1:123456789012:activity:testUser
                  .2016-10-27-18-11-35.f017c391-9363-481a-be2e-"
19     },
20     "responseElements": null,
21     "requestID": "490374ea-9cac-11e6-aed5-5b57d226e9ef",
22     "eventID": "e5eb9a3d-13bc-4fa1-9531-232d1914d263",
23     "eventType": "AwsApiCall",
24     "recipientAccountId": "123456789012"
25  }
```

DeleteStateMachine

The following example shows a CloudTrail log entry that demonstrates the DeleteStateMachine action:

```
1  {
2      "eventVersion": "1.04",
3      "userIdentity": {
4          "type": "IAMUser",
```

146

```json
5          "principalId": "AIDAJABK5MNKNAEXAMPLE",
6          "arn": "arn:aws:iam::123456789012:user/graphene/tests/test-user",
7          "accountId": "123456789012",
8          "accessKeyId": "AKIAJA2ELRVCPEXAMPLE",
9          "userName": "test-user"
10     },
11     "eventTime": "2016-10-28T01:17:37Z",
12     "eventSource": "states.amazonaws.com",
13     "eventName": "DeleteStateMachine",
14     "awsRegion": "us-east-1",
15     "sourceIPAddress": "10.61.88.189",
16     "userAgent": "Coral/Netty",
17     "errorCode": "AccessDenied",
18     "errorMessage": "User: arn:aws:iam::123456789012:user/graphene/tests/test-user is not
           authorized to perform: states:DeleteStateMachine on resource: arn:aws:states:us-east
           -1:123456789012:stateMachine:testUser.2016-10-27-18-16-38.ec6e261f-1323-4555-9fa",
19     "requestParameters": null,
20     "responseElements": null,
21     "requestID": "2cf23f3c-9cac-11e6-aed5-5b57d226e9ef",
22     "eventID": "4a622d5c-e9cf-4051-90f2-4cdb69792cd8",
23     "eventType": "AwsApiCall",
24     "recipientAccountId": "123456789012"
25 }
```

StartExecution

The following example shows a CloudTrail log entry that demonstrates the StartExecution action:

```json
1  {
2      "eventVersion": "1.04",
3      "userIdentity": {
4          "type": "IAMUser",
5          "principalId": "AIDAJYDLDBVBI4EXAMPLE",
6          "arn": "arn:aws:iam::123456789012:user/test-user",
7          "accountId": "123456789012",
8          "accessKeyId": "AKIAJL5C75K4ZEXAMPLE",
9          "userName": "test-user"
10     },
11     "eventTime": "2016-10-28T01:17:25Z",
12     "eventSource": "states.amazonaws.com",
13     "eventName": "StartExecution",
14     "awsRegion": "us-east-1",
15     "sourceIPAddress": "10.61.88.189",
16     "userAgent": "Coral/Netty",
17     "requestParameters": {
18         "input": "{}",
19         "stateMachineArn": "arn:aws:states:us-east-1:123456789012:stateMachine:testUser
               .2016-10-27-18-16-26.482bea32-560f-4a36-bd",
20         "name": "testUser.2016-10-27-18-16-26.6e229586-3698-4ce5-8d"
21     },
22     "responseElements": {
23         "startDate": "Oct 28, 2016 1:17:25 AM",
24         "executionArn": "arn:aws:states:us-east-1:123456789012:execution:testUser
               .2016-10-27-18-16-26.482bea32-560f-4a36-bd:testUser.2016-10-27-18-16-26.6e229586
```

```
            -3698-4ce5-8d"
25      },
26      "requestID": "264c6f08-9cac-11e6-aed5-5b57d226e9ef",
27      "eventID": "30a20c8e-a3a1-4b07-9139-cd9cd73b5eb8",
28      "eventType": "AwsApiCall",
29      "recipientAccountId": "123456789012"
30 }
```

StopExecution

The following example shows a CloudTrail log entry that demonstrates the StopExecution action:

```
1 {
2      "eventVersion": "1.04",
3      "userIdentity": {
4          "type": "IAMUser",
5          "principalId": "AIDAJYDLDBVBI4EXAMPLE",
6          "arn": "arn:aws:iam::123456789012:user/test-user",
7          "accountId": "123456789012",
8          "accessKeyId": "AKIAJL5C75K4ZEXAMPLE",
9          "userName": "test-user"
10     },
11     "eventTime": "2016-10-28T01:18:20Z",
12     "eventSource": "states.amazonaws.com",
13     "eventName": "StopExecution",
14     "awsRegion": "us-east-1",
15     "sourceIPAddress": "10.61.88.189",
16     "userAgent": "Coral/Netty",
17     "requestParameters": {
18         "executionArn": "arn:aws:states:us-east-1:123456789012:execution:testUser
                .2016-10-27-18-17-00.337b3344-83:testUser.2016-10-27-18-17-00.3a0801c5-37"
19     },
20     "responseElements": {
21         "stopDate": "Oct 28, 2016 1:18:20 AM"
22     },
23     "requestID": "4567625b-9cac-11e6-aed5-5b57d226e9ef",
24     "eventID": "e658c743-c537-459a-aea7-dafb83c18c53",
25     "eventType": "AwsApiCall",
26     "recipientAccountId": "123456789012"
27 }
```

Security

This section provides information about Step Functions security and authentication.

Topics

- Authentication
- Creating IAM Roles for AWS Step Functions
- Creating Granular IAM Permissions for Non-Admin Users

Step Functions uses IAM to control access to other AWS services and resources. For an overview of how IAM works, see Overview of Access Management in the *IAM User Guide*. For an overview of security credentials, see AWS Security Credentials in the Amazon Web Services General Reference.

Authentication

You can access AWS as any of the following types of identities:

- **AWS account root user** – When you first create an AWS account, you begin with a single sign-in identity that has complete access to all AWS services and resources in the account. This identity is called the AWS account *root user* and is accessed by signing in with the email address and password that you used to create the account. We strongly recommend that you do not use the root user for your everyday tasks, even the administrative ones. Instead, adhere to the best practice of using the root user only to create your first IAM user. Then securely lock away the root user credentials and use them to perform only a few account and service management tasks.

- **IAM user** – An IAM user is an identity within your AWS account that has specific custom permissions (for example, permissions to create a state machine in Step Functions). You can use an IAM user name and password to sign in to secure AWS webpages like the AWS Management Console, AWS Discussion Forums, or the AWS Support Center.

  In addition to a user name and password, you can also generate access keys for each user. You can use these keys when you access AWS services programmatically, either through one of the several SDKs or by using the AWS Command Line Interface (CLI). The SDK and CLI tools use the access keys to cryptographically sign your request. If you don't use AWS tools, you must sign the request yourself. Step Functions supports *Signature Version 4*, a protocol for authenticating inbound API requests. For more information about authenticating requests, see Signature Version 4 Signing Process in the *AWS General Reference*.

- **IAM role** – An IAM role is an IAM identity that you can create in your account that has specific permissions. It is similar to an *IAM user*, but it is not associated with a specific person. An IAM role enables you to obtain temporary access keys that can be used to access AWS services and resources. IAM roles with temporary credentials are useful in the following situations:

  - **Federated user access** – Instead of creating an IAM user, you can use existing user identities from AWS Directory Service, your enterprise user directory, or a web identity provider. These are known as *federated users*. AWS assigns a role to a federated user when access is requested through an identity provider. For more information about federated users, see Federated Users and Roles in the *IAM User Guide*.

  - **AWS service access** – You can use an IAM role in your account to grant an AWS service permissions to access your account's resources. For example, you can create a role that allows Amazon Redshift to access an Amazon S3 bucket on your behalf and then load data from that bucket into an Amazon Redshift cluster. For more information, see Creating a Role to Delegate Permissions to an AWS Service in the *IAM User Guide*.

- **Applications running on Amazon EC2** – You can use an IAM role to manage temporary credentials for applications that are running on an EC2 instance and making AWS API requests. This is preferable to storing access keys within the EC2 instance. To assign an AWS role to an EC2 instance and make it available to all of its applications, you create an instance profile that is attached to the instance. An instance profile contains the role and enables programs that are running on the EC2 instance to get temporary credentials. For more information, see Using an IAM Role to Grant Permissions to Applications Running on Amazon EC2 Instances in the *IAM User Guide*.

Creating IAM Roles for AWS Step Functions

AWS Step Functions can execute code and access AWS resources (such as invoking an AWS Lambda function). To maintain security, you must grant Step Functions access to those resources by using an IAM role.

The Tutorials in this guide enable you to take advantage of automatically generated IAM roles that are valid for the region in which you create the state machine. To create your own IAM role for a state machine, follow the steps in this section.

Create a Role for Step Functions

In this example, you create an IAM role with permission to invoke a Lambda function.

To create a role for Step Functions

1. Sign in to the IAM console, and then choose **Roles, Create role**.

2. On the **Select type of trusted entity** page, under **AWS service**, select **Step Functions** from the list and then choose **Next: Permissions**.

3. On the **Attached permissions policy** page, choose **Next: Review**.

4. On the **Review** page, type `StepFunctionsLambdaRole` for **Role Name**, and then choose **Create role**.

   The IAM role appears in the list of roles.

For more information about IAM permissions and policies, see Access Management in the *IAM User Guide*.

Creating Granular IAM Permissions for Non-Admin Users

The default managed policies in IAM, such as `ReadOnly`, don't fully cover all types of Step Functions permissions. This section describes these different types of permissions and provides some example configurations.

AWS Step Functions has four categories of permissions. Depending on what access you want to provide to a user, you can control access by using permissions in these categories.

Service-Level Permissions
Apply to components of the API that do not act on a specific resource.

State Machine-Level Permissions
Apply to all API components that act on a specific state machine.

Execution-Level Permissions
Apply to all API components that act on a specific execution.

Activity-Level Permissions
Apply to all API components that act on a specific activity or on a particular instance of an activity.

Service-Level Permissions

This permission level applies to all API actions that do not act on a specific resource. These include [CreateStateMachine](http://docs.aws.amazon.com/step-functions/latest/apireference/API_CreateStateMachine.html), [CreateActivity](http://docs.aws.amazon.com/step-functions/latest/apireference/API_CreateActivity.html), [ListStateMachines](http://docs.aws.amazon.com/step-functions/latest/apireference/API_ListStateMachines.html), and [ListActivities](http://docs.aws.amazon.com/step-functions/latest/apireference/API_ListActivities.html).

```
1  {
2    "Version": "2012-10-17",
3    "Statement": [
4      {
5        "Effect": "Allow",
6        "Action": [
7          "states:ListStateMachines",
8          "states:ListActivities",
9          "states:CreateStateMachine",
10         "states:CreateActivity"
11       ],
12       "Resource": [
13         "arn:aws:states:*:*:*"
14       ]
15     },
16     {
17       "Effect": "Allow",
18       "Action": [
19         "iam:PassRole"
20       ],
21       "Resource": [
22         "arn:aws:iam:::role/my-execution-role"
23       ]
24     }
25   ]
26 }
```

State Machine-Level Permissions

This permission level applies to all API actions that act on a specific state machine. These API require the ARN of the state machine as part of the request, such as [DeleteStateMachine](http://docs.aws.amazon.com/step-functions/latest/apireference/API_DeleteStateMachine.html), [DescribeStateMachine](http://docs.aws.amazon.com/step-functions/latest/apireference/API_DescribeStateMachine.html), [StartExecution](http://docs.aws.amazon.com/step-functions/latest/apireference/API_StartExecution.html), and [ListExecutions](http://docs.aws.amazon.com/step-functions/latest/apireference/API_ListExecutions.html).

```
1  {
2    "Version": "2012-10-17",
3    "Statement": [
4      {
5        "Effect": "Allow",
6        "Action": [
7          "states:DescribeStateMachine",
8          "states:StartExecution",
9          "states:DeleteStateMachine",
10         "states:ListExecutions",
11         "states:UpdateStateMachine"
12       ],
13       "Resource": [
14         "arn:aws:states:*:*:stateMachine:StateMachinePrefix*"
15       ]
16     }
17   ]
18 }
```

Execution-Level Permissions

This permission level applies to all the API actions that act on a specific execution. These API operations require the ARN of the execution as part of the request, such as [DescribeExecution](http://docs.aws.amazon.com/step-functions/latest/apireference/API_DescribeExecution.html), [GetExecutionHistory](http://docs.aws.amazon.com/step-functions/latest/apireference/API_GetExecutionHistory.html), and [StopExecution](http://docs.aws.amazon.com/step-functions/latest/apireference/API_StopExecution.html).

```
1  {
2    "Version": "2012-10-17",
3    "Statement": [
4      {
5        "Effect": "Allow",
6        "Action": [
7          "states:DescribeExecution",
8          "states:DescribeStateMachineForExecution",
9          "states:GetExecutionHistory",
10         "states:StopExecution"
11       ],
12       "Resource": [
13         "arn:aws:states:*:*:execution:*:ExecutionPrefix*"
14       ]
15     }
16   ]
17 }
```

Activity-Level Permissions

This permission level applies to all the API actions that act on a specific activity or on a particular instance of it. These API operations require the ARN of the activity or the token of the instance as part of the request, such as [DeleteActivity](http://docs.aws.amazon.com/step-functions/latest/apireference/API_DeleteActivity.html), [DescribeActivity](http://docs.aws.amazon.com/step-functions/latest/apireference/API_DescribeActivity.html), [GetActivityTask](http://docs.aws.amazon.com/step-functions/latest/apireference/API_GetActivityTask.html), [SendTaskSuccess](http://docs.aws.amazon.com/step-functions/latest/apireference/API_SendTaskSuccess.html), [SendTaskFailure](http://docs.aws.amazon.com/step-functions/latest/apireference/API_SendTaskFailure.html), and [SendTaskHeartbeat](http://docs.aws.amazon.com/step-functions/latest/apireference/API_SendTaskHeartbeat.html).

```
1  {
2    "Version": "2012-10-17",
3    "Statement": [
4      {
5        "Effect": "Allow",
6        "Action": [
7          "states:DescribeActivity",
8          "states:DeleteActivity",
9          "states:GetActivityTask",
10         "states:SendTaskSuccess",
11         "states:SendTaskFailure",
12         "states:SendTaskHeartbeat"
13       ],
14       "Resource": [
15         "arn:aws:states:*:*:activity:ActivityPrefix*"
16       ]
17     }
18   ]
19 }
```

Related Step Functions Resources

The following table lists related resources that you might find useful as you work with this service.

Resource	Description
AWS Step Functions API Reference	Descriptions of API actions, parameters, and data types and a list of errors that the service returns.
AWS Step Functions Command Line Reference	Descriptions of the AWS CLI commands that you can use to work with AWS Step Functions.
Product information for Step Functions	The primary web page for information about Step Functions.
Discussion Forums	A community-based forum for developers to discuss technical questions related to Step Functions and other AWS services.
AWS Premium Support Information	The primary web page for information about AWS Premium Support, a one-on-one, fast-response support channel to help you build and run applications on AWS infrastructure services.

Document History

This section lists major changes to the *AWS Step Functions Developer Guide*.

Latest documentation update: June 7, 2018

[See the AWS documentation website for more details]

AWS Glossary

For the latest AWS terminology, see the AWS Glossary in the *AWS General Reference*.